why sound matters

yale

university

press

new haven

and

london

damon

krukowski

why

sound

matters

"Why X Matters" is a registered trademark of Yale University.

Copyright © 2025 by Damon Krukowski. All rights reserved. This book may not be reproduced, in whole or in part, including illustrations, in any form (beyond that copying permitted by Sections 107 and 108 of the U.S. Copyright Law and except by reviewers for the public press), without written permission from the publishers.

Yale University Press books may be purchased in quantity for educational, business, or promotional use. For information, please e-mail sales.press@yale.edu (U.S. office) or sales@yaleup.co.uk (U.K. office).

Set in Adobe Garamond types by
Printed in the United States of America.

Library of Congress Control Number: 2025932265
ISBN 978-0-300-27224-6 (hardcover)

A catalogue record for this book is available from the British Library.

Authorized Representative in the EU: Easy Access System Europe, Mustamäe tee 50, 10621 Tallinn, Estonia, gpsr.requests@easproject.com.

10 9 8 7 6 5 4 3 2 1

also by damon krukowski

Ways of Hearing (2019)
The New Analog (2017)

But there is also an ecology of the world within our bodies.
—RACHEL CARSON, *Silent Spring*

contents

one Load-In 1

two Sound Is a Material 9

three Soundcheck 25

four Sound Has Value 33

five Backstage 49

six Music Is Labor 57

seven At the Merch Table 73

eight A Community Theory of Value 81

nine The Next Gig 95

Notes 109

Index 00

why sound matters

I load-in

As the worst of the COVID pandemic passed, I felt especially eager to get back to live music. My entire adult life has included music performance, not just my own but others', including most of my friends—I've likely spent more time in bars, clubs, and small theaters around the world than in any other public spaces as a result. There were many varied shocks to the lockdown of 2020, but for working musicians like me perhaps the greatest was the ban—100 percent—on live music.

Live music has since come back slowly, not all at once but in drips and drabs, attempts and failures. The "new normal" isn't normal to this day, at least to someone whose career in music started before the pandemic. Touring is freshly problematic for a number of reasons: risk of contagion, which still regularly causes illness and cancellations, but also elevated travel costs, the widespread loss of independent venues that couldn't wait out the lockdown, and changed audience habits. Many professionals left the business altogether, from tour-bus drivers to sound engineers to booking agents to musicians who decided they just couldn't anymore. In the United Kingdom, which keeps better official tabs on our industry than most places, 26 percent of jobs in music were lost between the start of the pandemic and its so-called end. That's 52,000 fewer people working in music, and that's just the U.K.[1]

My own touring restarted, but fitfully—it's possible that it may never return to what it was. So when I saw an ad to run the soundboard part-time at a club within walking distance of my home in Cambridge, Massachusetts, I thought, If I can't travel for live music as much as before, maybe I could engage with more of it that comes to my neighborhood.

The ad also caught my eye because it wasn't from just any local club; it was the storied Club Passim, formerly Club 47, which started in the late 1950s and still, incredibly, hosts live folk music seven nights a week in Harvard Square. Indeed, Passim has been a fixture for so long that I have lived in Cambridge since the 1980s and managed to ignore it almost entirely. It was never the new thing, naturally; and it never quite came back in fashion either. It just kept on keeping on, still mining the vein of music that it started with when Joan Baez, Bob Dylan, and so many others put this small coffeehouse on the map.

Over the years I had been to only a handful of shows at Passim, but each was memorable. Mostly I had gone to see a folky hero who was still playing the same circuit they had in the day. I had the privilege of seeing John Renbourn and Jacqui McShee, of the U.K. jazz-folk band Pentangle; the Jim Kweskin Jug Band, from the original Boston folk revival; and Tom Rapp of the psychedelic-folk band Pearls Before Swine, with whom my partner Naomi Yang and I toured in the late 1990s and who insisted on playing this particular venue when it came to choosing one in Boston or Cambridge. Tom introduced us to a few other folk clubs too, but afterwards we went back to playing "rock" rooms and still do, even though we are essentially an acoustic live act.

The instrumentation of my music did give me some qualifications for working sound at Passim, however; I know how to mic an acoustic guitar and vocals, as well as bass, drums, and all the other instruments we have toured with or that have appeared on our records, which share a sonic palette with much of the music that comes through folk clubs. So I applied, and a bit to my surprise was hired. I ran the soundboard there part-time for about a year and half.

What I found at Club Passim was more of what I missed from live music than I expected. Because the club isn't part of my circuit, or the circuit most of my friends play, I didn't always see the music there that I love the most. But the room is filled with sound and people sharing that sound, which is more of what I needed than I knew.

At the start of each of my shifts at Passim, the room was closed to the public as the musicians arrived for soundcheck. They went through all the mechanical movements of unpacking their gear that I know so well. We'd talk logistics—parking, meals, merch—

and we'd chat, because musicians are always good at hanging out. We'd talk about where they were last, where they are heading next, about who we know in common, about music we're listening to or who we saw play recently. And then we'd talk about their instruments, because I was going to mic them.

I loved this part of the job. Every instrument has a story. And every musician is ready to tell it.

Let me share a particularly great one—they aren't nearly all so dramatic, yet they often have a bit of the happenstance and magic in this tale.

The Canadian singer-songwriter James Keelaghan was unpacking his gear, comfortably settling back on a stage he'd been many times before—although this was his first visit since the pandemic lockdown. He took out a well-traveled acoustic guitar and held it in his lap. Then, with a throwaway tone, he said, Oh, do you mind if I play one song on a different guitar? You'll have to mic it up as well. Not at all, I said. So he took another out of its case and placed it behind him on a stand.

An off-stage choir might have started singing as I looked at that second guitar. It fairly glowed—with what I wasn't sure. It was a standard though clearly very old Martin parlor guitar, the small size favored back when folk instruments were made primarily for private settings rather than a public room like a bar or venue. Parlor guitars are "12-fret," meaning the neck meets the body where the octave on each open string repeats—no flashy leads way up the neck on guitars like this. They're made for quiet strumming or picking. It wasn't elaborately appointed, no fussy or fancy details. But it looked *taut,* somehow—like the wood was vibrating, and sound was already emanating from it as it sat on the stand.

"What is that," I said—My jaw might have been open as I did.

"Oh, it's got a story," said Keelaghan's bass player, David Woodhead, also busy unpacking his gear.

James Keelaghan is known in folk circles for his narrative songs. He's a great storyteller in lyric and naturally in conversation as well. He talks between tunes in his set, charming the audience with polished gems of anecdotes and jokes, making everyone feel like they're by the fire of an old pub in Ireland. Where—in a side hustle—he takes groups of tourists on trips.

The skilled storyteller quickly sized me up before he started. "That guitar," he said, "was at Pearl Harbor."

I was hooked.

The guitar was even older than I had imagined, bought new in 1905 by a woman who played it in her parlor, as intended. And when this woman's son wanted to see the world and enlisted in the navy, his mother gave him the guitar to take with him. But first she removed the thirteenth fret. For luck.

Keelaghan took out his phone and showed me a picture of a young sailor named Eugene Peck in his whites holding the guitar. It was poorly exposed and slightly out of focus, a snapshot from a Kodak Brownie, but there was a dark stripe on the neck of the guitar, just above where it met the body—the missing thirteenth fret.

This guitar went round the world with the sailor, Keelaghan said. He was crazy for slack-key music from Hawaii, and he eventually ended up stationed there on the USS *Nevada*.

Load-In 5

Now you know the *Nevada,* Keelaghan continued, with the tone of the history buff that he is, was the only battleship that managed to sortie on December 7, 1941. But this sailor didn't make it. Afterward, his shipmates collected his things and returned them to his mother. She put the guitar under her bed, where it stayed.

"But it has all its frets," I interrupted. Right on cue.

Keelaghan paused for breath and went on. So after this woman passed, a nephew found the guitar under the bed. He had it restored—the thirteenth fret was replaced—and kept it with him always. You know Pistol River Friendship Hall? Keelaghan suddenly asked me. This was a kind of question I got all the time when I was working sound at Passim, but I rarely knew the reference since I don't play the folk circuit. I shook my head and got a fresh lookover. Well, he went on, maybe a little more warily than before, Glenn Elfman there once asked me after a show—we were up late, drinking—he asked if I would play this song of mine, "Kiri's Piano," on an old guitar of his. Sure, I said.

Now, "Kiri's Piano," Keelaghan explained—I'll sing it later tonight so you'll hear it then—is a story I learned about a woman taken to a Japanese internment camp in British Columbia during the war. She played the piano. But when they went round her empty house to confiscate it, they found she had dumped the piano in the harbor rather than let anyone else have it.

So I sing him my song on his guitar. And only after I'm done does Glenn tell me the story of this instrument. Years later, after he died, I learned Glenn had willed it to me.

We all looked at the guitar in silence.

"How do you like it mic'ed," I asked, after a moment.

"I don't know," he said. "It's the first time I ever brought this guitar onstage."[2]

When I was asked to write a book about why sound matters, I thought of my recent experiences at Passim. The community there is built around music—a carefully, even conservatively defined style of music. But what holds it together isn't just the music, it's also something physical. You feel it in the room, and I believe that's what brings people back there as much as or possibly more than any given artist.

It was that physicality I had missed during the pandemic. We all heard recorded music throughout, as much as we wanted. Yet according to streaming stats, during lockdown people spent less time with music than usual, not more.[3] We weren't able to share sounds together in a physical space, and it seems we need to.

This book is an attempt to understand better what that material aspect of sound is about. Not from a scientific point of view—I was educated before the emphasis on STEM (science, technology, engineering, and math), so you'll need to go elsewhere for that kind of explanation. But there's another materiality to the world, the one that begins with our senses and our interactions with one another. You don't need specialized knowledge to understand that, you just need to be human. And musicians are humans who pay attention to sound every working day. It's part of the labor we do, along with packing and unpacking our gear.

2. sound is a material

Like other natural resources, sound is a material.

That feels intuitive to me, but I appreciate it needs explanation because sound is often understood, especially in the context of music, as precisely something that is *immaterial.* Consider the well-worn thought experiment: If a tree falls in the forest and there is no one to hear it, does it make a sound?

If sound is a material—like the wood of the tree, the earth it grows from, the air that surrounds it, the water that nourishes it, the fire that can consume it—then the answer is obvious: Yes. Of course there is sound in the forest, whether or not a person (or any animal, if you want to extend the courtesy to other beings with similar sense organs) is there to hear it.

Yet the riddle persists, because the idea of sound is so closely tied to our perception of it. Interaction with our bodies may be the only way most of us experience sound—but paradoxically this is the very reason it might seem to have no substance of its own. It is all around us, apparently without form.

The equally well-worn Zen koan might speak to this: What is the sound of one hand clapping? Or, to rephrase it in a parallel construction to the Western thought experiment: If one hand claps and no one can hear it, does it make a sound?

It is not unusual to include nominally mute gestures as a part of what we perceive as music. If you google the phrase "Music is what happens between the notes," you might find the quote credited to anyone from Claude Debussy to Duke Ellington, Miles Davis to Yo-Yo Ma, because it's a widely shared thought. But the Zen koan pushes beyond our ideas of music. Does an instrument at rest make a *sound?*

If sound is a material, then it is independent of our perception of it. We may not be able to perceive the sound of one hand clapping, or of an old Martin parlor guitar sitting on a stand, but that doesn't preclude the idea that it makes a sound regardless. The Zen koan, as I understand it, urges us to expand our idea of perception to include that possibility.

The sound of one hand clapping remains obscure, but the notion that it could make a sound is much the same as for the unobserved tree in the forest. Both are beyond our reach as limited observers. But so are some high frequencies in recorded music, to me and others my age. So are some recorded frequencies to all but mastering engineers with "golden ears," and manufacturers of expensive audio equipment (along with, if you believe them, their salespeople). Sound exists apart from our perception of it *because it is a material.*

There's a less philosophical path to this same conclusion, by tracing sound as a resource—a practice that I believe is increasingly urgent.

Our environment is often measured in terms of resources. We exploit the materials of the environment, for good and ill, and we are familiar with its elements not least through their compromise. Air pollution, water pollution, and soil contamination are evidence of the material world around us, as well as our dependence on it.

Noise pollution is less widely discussed at present, but we are all familiar with the concept. One of the foundational texts of modern environmentalism—*Silent Spring,* by Rachel Carson—uses *lack of sound* as an emblem for the damage humans have wrought on the environment. "The early mornings are strangely silent where once they were filled with the beauty of bird song," wrote Carson, painting a picture of death rather than life in the landscape.[1] Sound is embedded in our engagement with the material world and in our efforts to protect it from human degradation.

In current environmental literature, noise pollution is written about most often with regard to the ocean—a place where, it is interesting to note, humans cannot hear most sounds without technological assistance. Underwater is a vast world of trees falling with no people there to listen. Yet it is clear that sound in the ocean exists, is made use of by innumerable types of life, and is disrupted by human abuse of it.

That abuse is, like all contemporary abuses of the environment, extreme. A 2021 omnibus paper in *Science* magazine surveyed over ten thousand individual studies of marine acoustics and tallied damage to every level of sea life. "Over the past 50 years, increased shipping has contributed an estimated 32-fold increase in the low-frequency noise present along major shipping routes," report the twenty-five authors of the article, raising the alarm. "Human activity has altered biophony and geophony and has, either deliberately or as a by-product, added an increasingly prevalent third component—anthrophony—across a broad range of frequencies to ocean soundscapes."[2]

Anthrophony in the sea does not refer to the presence of people, who make little sound underwater, but to the presence of human industry. The constant pursuit of fossil fuel is a major part of this altered ocean soundscape—unsurprising, given its foundational role in modern pollution of all kinds.

> Examples of deliberate human use of marine sound include seismic surveys that produce high-energy, low-frequency, short-duration sounds aimed at detecting the presence of petroleum and gas deposits below the seafloor, as well as multibeam echosounders and side-scan sonars that generally produce high-frequency sounds to map the seabed and detect organisms and particles in the water column. These sensing techniques are, at times, a major component of present ocean soundscapes in many areas, especially those holding oil and gas reservoirs. . . . Similarly, construction and operation of oil and gas infrastructure (e.g., platforms, pipelines) increase anthrophony. The dynamic positioning systems (i.e.,

propellers and thrusters) used to maintain the position of offshore structures, such as drilling platforms, produce low-frequency noise.[3]

Additional extractive activities—mining, industrial fishing—contribute to the underwater cacophony:

> Technology that scrapes the bottom of the ocean—whether dredging the seafloor, harvesting minerals, or trawling for fisheries—also generates low-frequency noise. Dynamite fishing, designed to stun or kill reef fish for easy collection, remains a major source of blasting noise in Southeast Asia and coastal Africa.

Not to mention that most characteristically human activity, war:

> Controlled detonation of bombs dropped on the seafloor during World War II continues, more than 70 years later, to be a major source of disruptive and destructive sound in the North Sea. Explosions of mines, missiles, and bombs during naval warfare or military exercises also represent a source of destructive sound.

The effect on life in the ocean of all this human-produced noise is wide and deep. The authors of the paper cite "the pervasive and prevalent impacts of chronic exposure to noise across vast spans of the ocean" with corresponding "impacts of anthropogenic noise on fishes, invertebrates, and whole marine ecosystems." This damage is multifold: "Noise has been reported to disrupt traveling, foraging, socializing, communicating, resting, and other behaviors in marine mammals; attenuate antipredator behavior of young fishes, leading to increased mortality and reduced ability to learn to avoid predators in future encounters; and impact the settlement and development of invertebrates."

Like other environmental damage, noise in the ocean creates a feedback loop. As the natural sound environment is reduced by loss of marine life and ecosystems due to noise, the prevalence of human-made sound in the ocean increases, which leads to further degradation of life in the sea, and so on.

The disastrous noise pollution of the oceans makes clear that sound is a natural resource. Sound is among the materials of the world, not some property of humanity pinned to our perceptions. We may not be able to hear all the sounds of the sea, but we can destroy them.

Similar to other pollution, noise in the sea is only partly the result of deliberate human use of sound—the rest is a by-product, discarded into the environment without containment or sufficient concern. The purpose of shipping is not to generate noise. Nonetheless it leaves an audio wake, emanating out and down and poisoning the existing soundscape.

Noise as a by-product of technology—a waste product—is another example of the materiality of sound. Yet because sound is often regarded as immaterial, the effect of this waste is rarely measured. Were sound solid, like the garbage we pile into landfills, cities like New York and Tokyo would be buried beneath audio accumulation. Were it liquid, those cities would have drowned far in advance of sea rise from climate change. Were it gas or fire, they would be abandoned.

But sound seems to flow around us, no matter how dense it becomes. And so we let it accumulate. And accumulate. And accumulate. Just as we have in the ocean.

"There are no places on Earth that I've been that haven't been affected by human sound," says Bernie Krause, the eminent field recordist and soundscape ecologist.[4] Gordon Hempton, writer and recordist, has been advocating for the preservation of quiet places, and his organization QPI (Quiet Parks International) maintains a map pinpointing the precious few "certified" locations around the globe—I count only nine currently listed in the United States. Just as in the oceans, it's vehicular traffic that eliminates most places from that list. Les Blomberg of the advocacy group Noise Pollution Clearinghouse cites this striking figure: "In 1900, 20–25% of the continental US was impacted by vehicle noise; in 2000, 97.4% was impacted. Planes finished the task of destroying natural quiet in the second half of the 20th century, flying over the few remaining quiet areas."[5]

Airplanes do not exist to generate sound any more than ships do. But their waste product has thoroughly littered the globe. If we can count the few places on earth or sea without human-generated sound, it is effectively too late to talk about noise pollution. The planet is saturated with human sound. Natural biophony without humans has reached the point of near extinction.

And yet it seems we still don't notice how extreme this pollution has become. Perhaps we do not notice because we were all born well into the era of widespread vehicular traffic and have never known anything else.

During my lifetime, noise pollution has increased not because of any particular new invention or industrial practice but simply alongside a dramatic increase in the population, which has more than doubled since the 1960s. There has been a corresponding increase in the number of cars and trucks and planes, and in the density of our cities. The technology responsible for noise pollution was all in place by the mid-twentieth century; there was just a lot less of it.

In 1962, when Rachel Carson wrote *Silent Spring,* she heard nothing where there was no biological life due to DDT poisoning. By 1989, when Bill McKibben wrote his landmark climate-change book *The End of Nature,* he went into the woods by his home and heard . . . a chainsaw.

"Now that we have changed the most basic forces around us, the noise of that chainsaw will always be in the woods," he wrote. "Even in the most remote wilderness, where the strictest laws forbid the felling of a single tree, the sound of that saw will be clear, and a walk in the woods will be changed—tainted—by its whine."[6]

McKibben is speaking metaphorically here, at least in part; what was important to him in 1989 was that "an idea, a relationship, can go extinct" and that idea is "nature" isolated from humans. But he really did hear a chainsaw in the woods by his mountain home. And today in the twenty-first century, according to globetrotting sound recordists and ecologists like Bernie Krause and Gordon Hempton, any rhetorical exaggeration of McKibben's has been overtaken by reality. There truly is the sound of a chainsaw—or at least an airplane—in every location, no matter how remote. There is no more aural wilderness. There is no "silent" spring, even where we have killed off other life, because human sounds are everywhere.

When noise pollution is raised as an issue in contemporary environmental literature, the context is usually health—sometimes of animals, in particular sea mammals, but mostly human health. The United Nations Environment Programme (UNEP) included a special section on noise pollution in its 2022 report and framed it this way:

Today, noise pollution is a major environmental problem, cited as a top environmental risk to health across all age and social groups and an addition to the public health burden. Prolonged exposure to high levels of noise impairs human health and well-being, which is a growing concern for both the public and policymakers.

This "environmental risk to health" is explained in terms of human exposure to loud noise, either sudden or sustained.

Physically, proximity to very loud abrupt sounds, such as a gunshot over 140 dB [decibels], could rupture the ear's tympanic membrane, causing immediate hearing loss. Listening to music with earphones at the maximum volume—ranging between 90 and 100 dB at the eardrum—could start to cause hearing damage after only 15 minutes per day. Regular exposure to over 85 dB for an 8-hour day or longer can cause permanent hearing damage. Long-term exposures, even at relatively lower noise levels that are common in urban areas, can also damage both physical and mental health.[7]

These specific health risks are detailed, in turn, by a World Health Organization (WHO) study undertaken in Europe in order to "develop guidelines and provide recommendations for protecting human health from exposure to environmental noise."

The health outcomes include annoyance; cardiovascular and metabolic effects; cognitive impairment; effects on sleep; hearing impairment and tinnitus; adverse birth outcomes; and quality of life, mental health and well-being. The noise sources considered in these reviews include road traffic, railways, aircraft, wind turbines, and leisure activities such as attending sporting or concert events, listening to music through personal devices, and other recreational pastimes.[8]

A list of environmental problems that starts with "annoyance" doesn't seem particularly urgent, given the current state of our

Sound Is a Material

planet. And while the WHO documents actual threats to human life due to noise, the statistic it highlights is an estimated twelve thousand annual premature deaths in Europe connected to stresses such as loss of sleep. Noise exposure is seen as one "risk factor" out of many that contribute to "the development of cardiovascular and metabolic disorders such as elevated blood pressure, arterial hypertension, coronary heart disease and diabetes."

To put this risk in perspective against other environmental dangers, scientists led by the Barcelona Institute for Global Health calculated that over sixty-one thousand people died in Europe from the excessive heat of 2022. UNICEF and the WHO estimated forty-three thousand deaths due to drought that same year in Somalia alone.[9] Floods, crop failures, and desertification are currently threatening millions upon millions of lives around the globe due to climate emergencies. Annoyance from excess noise levels, even if it leads to higher blood pressure and stresses on the heart and circulatory system, doesn't really rank.

Which is not to say that noise pollution isn't a serious problem—I am writing about it because I believe it is. But justifying our attention to this pollution by appealing to human health is likely the reason there are hardly any entries for "noise" in indexes of books devoted to the climate emergency. While the earth is burning, complaints about noise levels seem rather minor, even a bit NIMBY ("not in my backyard").

The NIMBY aspect of responses to noise pollution is especially apparent when potential solutions to reducing carbon emissions—such as wind turbines—generate sound of their own. Where I live in Massachusetts, there has been an extended battle between environmentalists pushing wind power, on the one hand, and conservationists protecting the sea where turbines are installed, on the other. Add owners of leisure boats and desirable oceanside property to the mix, and you see where this leads. Do we take noise complaints about wind turbines seriously, or do we treat them as an "annoyance" for people lucky enough to have ocean views?

On a smaller scale, an appeal to the effect on human health can be used to justify noise complaints that might otherwise be dismissed as minor quality-of-life issues. In my town, Cambridge, attempts to limit or ban the use of leaf blowers went nowhere until local advocates enlisted doctors to testify that the dust they raise threatens the health of children and the immunocompromised. Now we have restrictions on these noxious machines at all times near playgrounds and schools, and seasonally throughout the city. But it was never enough to point out they simply make too much noise.

After all, our society has many positive associations with noise as a marker of economic dynamism and growth. Construction noise has limits nearly everywhere people live, though not nearly enough to constrain development—that would be much harder to push through a city council than restrictions on leaf blowers. Quiet would seem to be a goal for residents of every locale. However, not when put up against increased property values, tax bases, and services. Enter the jackhammers, pile drivers, heavy machinery, and trucks that turn economically "healthy" neighborhoods into deafening construction sites, at least during permitted hours.

Sound Is a Material

Quiet is becoming a luxury in our cities, available mainly to those who can afford soundproofing as part of what is being built with all that noisy construction. In New York City, high-end buildings are installing windows that cost a minimum of two thousand dollars apiece in order to seal apartments off from exterior noise. Windows like these aren't meant to be opened; at most they are "semi-operable," capable of opening only a bit if necessary. Instead, air is provided by ventilation systems.

The net result is a living space so insulated against exterior sound that it can become unnerving for its occupants. As one acoustical consultant explained to *New York* magazine, "You don't necessarily want super-high-performing windows for a condo in a quiet neighborhood. It makes the interior noise levels too quiet."[10]

Meanwhile, noise levels on the street—and inside less luxurious living spaces—continue to ramp up. Contributing to noise pollution are the very machines used to ventilate, heat, and cool the sheltered interiors of buildings. Even in my New England town, many more homes have recently added central air conditioning with exterior compressors as climate change has made it harder to simply throw open the windows and turn on a fan for hot summer days. An increasing number are also installing heat pumps to the outside of their homes, because these present a more energy-efficient means of regulating interior temperatures throughout the year. In both cases—air conditioning is grossly polluting and accounts for an estimated 4 percent of all greenhouse gas emissions, while heat pumps are touted as an environmentally conscious choice—the noise level around these buildings has increased exponentially because of the new machines.[11] In the United Kingdom, where an ambitious government program has set a goal of installing six hundred thousand heat pumps a year toward the elimination of oil burners by 2035, it has been pointed out that in practice the majority of installed heat pumps violate the government's own noise ordinances.[12] Yet residents of homes with heat pumps are less likely to notice the problem themselves, now that they keep their windows closed year round.

This split between interior and exterior soundscape is fast becoming the norm not only in famously loud places like New York City but in smaller towns and even in suburbs once known for their bucolic atmosphere. It may look quiet out on the lawn seen through plate glass. In truth, it's awash in noise from compressors and generators ringing the house and the neighbors' houses. Not to mention leaf blowers.

Were we to accept sound as a material and a natural resource *for its own sake*—not only for the sake of human health, or the health of other large mammals—perhaps we might see this walling off from sound differently. Homes insulated from the exterior soundscape function suspiciously like cars. Once they are sealed up, generating noise on the outside without regard for conditions on the street, consuming energy to maintain their interior comfort, they begin to resemble even larger versions of the SUVs parked in their driveways and garages.

Sound may be the easiest element of the environment to isolate. As we all experienced during the COVID pandemic, it is nearly impossible to isolate oneself from shared air. Water and earth are even more difficult—not that billionaires planning a future on Mars aren't starting to try. But sound is relatively simple to control. And many of us are already well on our way to living in a thoroughly controlled sound environment.

If you live in a house with the windows pulled shut, enter your car with windows rolled up, drive to a place where the windows are sealed, and then get back in the car to go back to the house, how much do you interact with the exterior soundscape? Earbuds are the portable version of this isolation, for pedestrians and riders of public transportation. And there is a feedback loop to this behavior, like with other environmental damage: as the soundscape deteriorates fewer elect to share in it, encouraging its further degradation.

Devices used for audio isolation are technological solutions to problems generated by other technology. It isn't birdsong or the patter of rain we try to keep from entering our homes, it's the sound of machinery and vehicles. One obvious solution would be to reduce the number of machines and vehicles around us—but most solutions pursued today with capital and vigor only generate more technology instead. Even if that technology contributes to the original problem.

This is emblematic of the way we are failing to address our environmental problems at large. Sound might seem low stakes by comparison with carbon emissions in the air, plastics in the water, or toxic chemicals in the land. But the mechanism is the same. Perhaps the stakes in noise pollution aren't so low as we assume, because all of the environment is tied together. As is all human behavior with regard to the environment.

The good news is that just as sound is the easiest element to wall oneself off from in a poisoned environment, it is also the easiest isolation to undo. Imagine, for example, that we all opened our windows (at least those of us who still have fully operable ones) and took joint responsibility for what we heard outside. Isn't that precisely what we need to do for our air, water and earth as well? Break our isolation from the shared environment that we in fact depend on.

"Borrowed scenery" or "borrowed landscape" is a traditional garden design principle from China and Japan, where framing, echoing, or otherwise responding to a view beyond a garden's walls is made part of the garden itself. In truth there is no garden without a borrowed view, at least of the sky. But acknowledging and honoring the connection between the garden within one's reach and the landscape beyond puts the two in deliberate dialogue. It is the opposite of walling oneself off, even if a wall is what defines the garden.

In audio matters, we tend not to honor the borrowed soundscape. I sit in my backyard on certain mornings and curse the leaf blower used by the church across the street to clear its parking lot of dust.

But in the evening, after the construction pickups have left and rush-hour traffic subsides, it is eerily still. Only a decade or so ago, our back garden was filled at all times of day and night with the motion and sounds of insects—it took just a little quiet beyond the garden, in the borrowed soundscape, to help me tune in to their activity. No longer. We have some bees attracted to our flowers. There are some ants moving from here to there. And in August, thank god, we still host crickets. But there is no haze of constant activity and buzz throughout the warmer months, as before.

This "insect apocalypse" is being documented by scientists measuring biomass—researchers in New Hampshire have reported an 80 percent drop in beetles since the 1970s; in Germany, scientists found a 76 percent reduction in the number of all flying insects since 1989; and in England, a 65 percent reduction in "splat rate" on vehicle number plates since just 2004, roughly the same period Naomi and I have been cultivating our own back garden.[13] The audio impact of this reduction in insect life is harder to measure, but undoubtedly the loss has been shared by all hearing observers during this drop-off. The soundscape inside walled gardens has become quieter, as the borrowed soundscape has grown louder.

Yet still we hold on to an ideal of isolation for audio. Might it be that if we gave that up—were we to acknowledge more fully the borrowed soundscape as an integral part of our audio experiences—we might then take greater responsibility for the communal soundscape?

Sound is a material, and it is a human failing not to see the value in that natural resource, just as it is a failing not to value the air, water, and earth. Which might well be our undoing as a species.

So listen up.

3 soundcheck

Getting behind the soundboard at Club Passim was a change of perspective for me in performance spaces. As the audio engineer, I was now the one who got the complaint "more low end in the guitar" from a veteran performer who always strums way up the neck, where there is no resonance in the low end of an acoustic guitar. I ran the board for some remarkable players, and I learned from the wide variety of approaches they take to their instruments and voices. But I also saw how sometimes habits—especially those formed early in a career—can stick regardless of their usefulness to the current situation. Drummers don't always play to the room, in particular; it's hard for some to adjust dynamics if their stage techniques have been honed under larger, louder circumstances. But it's not just drummers—a vocalist with a long background in rock clubs might habitually step back from the mic, tighten their throat, and deliver a Springsteen-like shout all evening long, even in a coffeehouse built for Joan Baez. It can work the other way around, too; some folk players don't address microphones or the sound system at all, having come up in truly acoustic rooms. One famous older folk singer I worked with told me to take the mic away from his mouth—"I sing to my audience," he explained, as I lowered it, and lowered it, and lowered it until he signaled it was perfect down by his Adam's apple. Bluegrass players—and there are a lot of excellent ones on the folk circuit these days—frequently ask to play into one condenser mic placed center stage, as in black-and-white photos of the Grand Ole Opry. That works fine for those who understand this antique approach to sound reinforcement. But some then wander all over the place during their show, facing different sides of the room as they solo out of range from any amplification—assuming the mic will follow them as it does when they plug in, which they clearly usually do.

Listening to the space you're in for music may be natural from the audience's side of the stage, but many performers are used to an audio bubble. On bigger stages, there isn't a choice—sometimes you can't hear anything of the sound system that's placed between you and the audience, even if you're in a room that's not much bigger than a folk club. Down the block from Passim, in the five-hundred-person-capacity rock club the Sinclair (owned and operated by Bowery Presents/AEG), I saw Taja

Cheek from L'Rain walk to the lip of the stage and pivot a PA speaker toward herself in the middle of a show. She was trying to hear what the audience was hearing, she explained to me later. Taja wanted to share the sonic space with her listeners more than the technology in that room permitted. Outdoor festivals are the most extreme example of this divide, where there are no walls at all for sound to bounce off back to the musicians—the "inside sound," as my Japanese friends call a monitor mix onstage, is the only amplified sound the musicians can possibly hear. And it's a sound heard only by the musicians.

In pre-smartphone-mediated days, it was not unusual to feel shocked by the sound of one's own recorded voice. "Is that me?" we might say when an answering machine or other tape device first entered our lives. Our voices are the ur-inside sound—they feel different from within our bodies, where we hear additional vibrations conducted through our bones, than to others, who hear them only through their eardrums. And recording puts us in the position of others.

The first time my band Galaxie 500 entered a professional recording studio, in 1988, we were wholly unprepared for this experience of hearing what we sounded like from the outside, as it were. For a rock drummer, the disjuncture between the way music sounds from your chair behind the kit and the way it sounds to others is particularly stark. Sitting on top of the loudest instrument onstage, I hear a hierarchy of sounds upside down from the way an audience typically receives them: drums first; bass next; then midrange instruments like guitars or keys; and finally a distant voice, almost as an atmospheric element rather than the

Soundcheck 27

main event. Lyrics? I forever mishear them from behind the drums. Back in Galaxie 500, I often had no idea what lyrics my bandmate Dean Wareham was singing until we got into the studio and I suddenly heard them the way an audience would.

But it isn't just relative volume between instruments that changes in recording. It's a change of perspective, similar to moving from the stage to the audience. When sounds are mixed to emanate from a pair of speakers, their spatial relationship to one another is determined by audio engineers and producers, not the players. It is an artifact of the recording process.

Everything about recording is artifice—it is a constructed sound world. In the case of Galaxie 500, that construction was very clearly the work of a single person: our engineer and producer Kramer (he went by only one name), who was also the only employee in the studio he owned, Noise New York. We were a trio as a band; Kramer, as a producer, was very much a solo act. "It's like flying," he once said to us, gesturing toward the panel of instruments in front of him, lit up as in a cockpit. At Noise New York, I don't think anyone other than Kramer was even allowed to touch that equipment except the maintenance person who periodically came to check all the machines' functionality. And whoever that was must not have been given much time or many resources, because for the three years and three albums we made at Noise New York, Kramer's sixteen-track studio was, in effect, fifteen tracks—one channel remained forever broken.

Kramer's sound world was unmistakably a creation of Kramer's. He didn't try to make all the bands that came through Noise New York sound the same—how could he, as he once told us, since they each brought different instruments with them? But he constructed an atmosphere with those varied sounds that could only have emanated from his particular sensibility, and his pot-saturated control room. Sitting in the booth while Kramer mixed was like sitting inside his head, hearing the music conducted through bones as well as eardrums.

Recording in a studio was also a direct encounter—in what we didn't know then to distinguish as "real time," because there was no other—with at least one listener from outside the band. In our case, that listener was Kramer, who never tried to hide his instantaneous reactions to our music. When we played something that bored him, he would take out a box of Q-Tips and start laboriously cleaning his mixing desk. When we played something that interested him, even if it was by mistake, he would prick up his ears and refuse to tape another take. "Next!" he would shout in our headphones. Our recordings were already an encounter with an audience, long before we played them for anyone. They were a dialogue between our band and Kramer—who not only heard us from the outside, but was in control of how we would then sound to all others.

When we arrived at Noise New York to record our third and what turned out to be final Galaxie 500 album, Kramer's control room was unexpectedly missing. The New York City Fire Department had come for an inspection, declared the booth counter to code, and torn down its walls. Kramer's mixing desk was now barely separated from the rest of the studio. He said it wouldn't make a difference, but it did—that little smoke-filled booth had been exposed to air, and the bone conduction inside it seemed compromised. Our third album sounded markedly different to many listeners on release. Most assumed it was the band going through changes, which wasn't wrong. But what they couldn't know was how much Kramer's studio had changed, and with it the sound world of our recordings.

Studios like Kramer's Noise New York are now a rarity. Digital tools have made it far easier to record oneself rather than hire a studio and encounter a strange new sound world created by a strange new collaborator. If every musician with a digital audio workstation (DAW) could become their own Kramer, our recorded sound world would be only more eccentric and more diverse. I don't find that to be the case, unfortunately. Working alone is never the same as working with others. And drop-down menus with presets make it easy to sound "professional" by sounding the same as everyone else, not different. We didn't have that option when we started recording; matching widely known commercial sounds at the time would have taken resources far beyond our means, as well as beyond Kramer's technical reach.

Yet Kramer, for all his idiosyncratic approaches to recording, was very much a professional—he worked full time as a musician, audio engineer, and record producer. He spent every working minute with sound, and he made a living from it. This is precisely what digital tools, for all their dissemination of "professional" results, cannot replicate. They have in fact made it harder for those of us in recorded audio to make our work a profession. The reason is that digital media have changed the value of recorded music. And by change, I mean eliminate.

The elimination of value for recorded music matters to every working artist. To every listener, less so. I don't think that's for lack of empathy, or a lack of interest in artists' lives—fans care passionately about music and its creators. Rather, I think it's that we never really came to an agreement as a society about what the value of recorded music is, or should be. Not because we don't value music, but because we don't know how to assign economic value to sound.

4 sound has value

Sound is a material and therefore has value, like all materials in the environment. However, no one seems to know what that value is.

There is no commodity trading for sound, as for minerals from the earth. There are no territorial rights, as on the sea.

Since the invention of recording, it might seem like copyright creates private ownership of sounds—a version of real estate. But the sounds themselves are not strictly what anyone can claim rights over, as one would do for a piece of land. Recordings have a complicated copyright history, in part because sound remains elusive as property. In the United States, the Supreme Court ruled early on that everything *but* the sound on recordings might be subject to ownership: the disc, the paper label, the song, the technology that plays back the song . . . but not the sound. Sound is not a "tangible thing," ruled the Court in 1908. As a result, it wasn't until 1972 that U.S. law extended any kind of copyright over sound recordings—and once peer-to-peer file-sharing software Napster launched in 1999, it quickly became unclear whether that copyright had real meaning.

Today, the value of digital recordings is near or at zero. As for the physical embodiments of recordings, no one seems sure what they are worth any longer. CDs are worth nothing—they are literally left out with the trash in my neighborhood—until you are looking for one in particular which is inevitably $50 plus shipping on the internet marketplace Discogs. LPs are not much more predictable. Shops frequented by vinyl collectors have not only high-priced albums but also dollar bins filled with equally functional pressings, and trash piles of more in the back. In other words, it's not the *sound* that determines the value of these objects, just as the Supreme Court intuited in 1908. It's everything else.

Nevertheless, it's easy to find statements about the immeasurable value of music. "No Music, No Life" was the old Tower Records slogan—before the company went bankrupt. You might say music is truly "invaluable." It is simultaneously beyond value, and without any.

For musicians, how to monetize sound recordings in the digital era has been a puzzle for decades now. In the analog era, physical media for sound seemed to have a clear exchange value, like any object in the marketplace. However, that was a short-lived moment; it barely made it through half a century sandwiched between the heyday of radio and the advent of streaming. (In the United States, neither terrestrial radio nor digital streaming pays musicians directly for their sound recordings, and access to these sounds for listeners is largely free.)

It may be a sorry fact of capitalism, but without a way to value sound in the marketplace, sound goes largely unprotected by interests with power. Fortunes are built—and are being built—on products and services that make use of sound. But it isn't sound itself that provides the profit. Digital streaming, for example, uses sound to attract users to its platforms and to keep them there, then monetizes the *users* by brokering their time and data to advertisers and others. Live performance remains a mainstay for musicians and the largely corporate promoters who profit from their appearances, but, again, it isn't the sound itself being sold so much as the presence of a performer in a particular place at a given time. The ticket is what has exchange value, rented access to a space, just like any other real estate negotiation.

When sound is marketed for its own sake, its value is often discussed in terms of human health—similar to the way noise pollution is discussed though with a positive spin rather than negative. The current vogue for "sound baths" values sound as healing vibration. Muzak—that old-fashioned, anonymous background music once played in shopping centers and dentists' offices—and its successor, streaming platform playlists based on mood, are similar to sound baths in that their value is measured by an effect on the body. These are examples of sound as a drug—whether analgesic, narcotic, amphetamine, aphrodisiac, or some combination—with a clear use and therefore a measurable value. On the streaming service Spotify in 2022, "white noise and ambient podcasts accounted for 3 million daily consumption hours on the platform," according to internal corporate documents leaked to Bloomberg News. Those are user hours Spotify would like to capture for sounds it doesn't need to license, these documents revealed, potentially boosting its annual profit by $38 million.[1]

It is relatively simple for a corporation like Spotify to take over a pharmaceutical use of sound from others because, as with a generic drug, there is no patent on white noise or the patter of rain. Coopting sounds from an artist is another matter—not only because an artist's work is tied to copyright, but, I would venture, because no one knows what its value truly is. If a sound can put people to sleep, or make them focus as they work, it has a use that might be duplicated in myriad ways and consequently measured economically against them. If sound moves listeners as an artist's can—that is, in ways that cannot be fully anticipated or predicted, or even sufficiently explained—its results can't be reproduced by other means. Its value remains entirely up to individuals, each of whom may assign it wildly different worth.

This might explain why the prices of CDs and LPs are bouncing around crazily at present. In the digital era, these media have no intrinsic value other than the cost of their physical materials (falling toward zero for CDs, increasingly expensive for LPs). And the sounds on them generally do not come with a use value, like the white noise that draws three million daily consumption hours on Spotify. If a musician can attract equivalent attention on a streaming platform to white noise, their recordings are valued highly for the moment—but those same sounds will carry no value once that attention dissipates. White noise, on the other hand, is forever.

Putting human health aside—all the positive effects on our bodies from sound, all the negative ones from noise pollution—do we have another way to determine the value of sound? I believe we do, but it goes largely unremarked by consumers and is sometimes deliberately dismissed by corporations. That value is labor.

Just as sound is a material in the environment, it is a material subject to human labor. White noise might seem labor-free—precisely why Spotify resents paying anyone for having uploaded it to the platform. The same holds for sounds of rain, or ocean waves, or wind, or all the many natural sounds so useful to our bodies. But once these sounds are recorded, they have been subjected to human labor. And labor has value. A value we can determine, and a value we can calculate.

Here we find a value for sound outside its use, whether as a drug or a work of art or both. Recording provides one clear link to labor. So does performance. So does curation. So does, it turns out, any and all work that humans do to share sounds with one another. Even streaming.

As sound studies scholar Jonathan Sterne wrote in *The Audible Past,* his influential account of the earliest days of sound recording, "Recording . . . does not preserve a preexisting sonic event as it happens so much as it creates and organizes sonic events for the possibility of preservation and repetition."[2] Consider a field recording of rain—one of the ambient sounds attracting so many listeners to Spotify each day. The sound of rain happens whether we hear it or not, because sound is a material in the environment independent from our perception of it. However, rain is not a "sonic event," to use Sterne's terminology, until a recordist makes it one. Another way to put this might be: there is no recording without labor. Sound recordings don't just happen.

Field recordings of nature demonstrate this especially well, because they don't depend on people generating the sounds they record. And yet people are clearly involved. How else do you get a recording? At minimum, someone must place a microphone somewhere. And that minimum already represents maximal human intervention: it is an act tied to technology, history, politics, economics, and—not least—art. There are choices to be made all along the path to recording, and those choices are framed by the fullness of human society.

If you have never tried placing a microphone somewhere yourself, think about how you use a smartphone. It has simple buttons to start and stop recording audio, image, or a combination of the two via video. But *when* you choose to use those buttons, *what* you choose to use them for, and whether or how you choose to *share* that content are decisions framed by personal and social considerations. That's without editing, or filters, or adding contextual statements—the decisions multiply as the process continues. And this is just for an Instagram post.

Now consider the field recordist at work. There is the decision of where or what is worth recording. There is the strategizing of how best to record it. There is the act of recording itself. Inevitably, there is the judgement of what in a given recording has more value and what has less—through the simple act of labeling a recording, if not also excerpting and/or editing it—in order to highlight that value for others.

Every step of this process entails human labor.

When Spotify conspires to use its own ambient recordings in place of those posted on its site, it is exercising its corporate power as a platform to supplant the labor of others. Three million daily hours of consumption, or $38 million of potential annual profit, have already been attracted to the platform by that labor—which Spotify would like to claim for itself by asserting there is no difference between various recordings of rain, or waves, or birds, or anything else in nature that we cannot easily identify as individual. And yet the labor represented by each of those recordings is highly individualized. It came from different people.

There's another, perhaps more surprising way that sound recordings of nature are tied to human labor. Because we have difficulty differentiating among individual instances of natural occurrences—one wave from the next, one robin call from another—audio recordings for nature documentaries are rarely recorded in sync with their images. Indeed, they are often not recorded in the field at all.

Graham Wild, sound mixer for many of the famous David Attenborough nature documentaries, explains:

> Ninety-nine percent of the time, it's shot mute. A lot of things are shot off-speed. They use very long lenses. They use various devices to get lovely tracking shots—they use helicopters, they use drones, all sorts of stuff—and all those aren't very good for sound, because you hear them a lot more than you do the animal or whatever it is that's a long way away. So we spend a lot of time trying to re-create

what you would hear if you were there. So it's very similar to drama, in that respect. It's kind of a bit different to normal documentary, where you start with sound that's been recorded of people talking and you add things to it. In natural history, you tend to start with nothing.[3]

Among nature documentarians, it seems to be a point of pride that when vocal calls are used—from birds or animals—they should be accurate at least to the species, drawn from a library of existing field recordings. But many of the creatures on-screen do not vocalize in a manner accessible to humans. For those, as well as to enhance natural soundscapes, documentarians routinely turn to foley.

Foley is a sound art named after an early practitioner, Jack Foley, who provided audio effects for some of the first talkie films in Hollywood. It has its roots in theater and on radio, but is primarily associated with film, where it continues to play a crucial role. Footsteps are a classic foley addition to film—because if you think about it, what microphone is going to pick up the sounds of someone's feet? Yet as viewers we have come to expect footsteps with nearly every movement of a body on-screen, even nonhuman ones.

Our association of movement with sound leads nature documentarians to use foley despite its clearly nondocumentary qualities. "You can fill a television screen with a shot of a spider walking across a web, and there's no sound there, obviously," says Richard Hinton, a prominent foley artist who specializes in nature documentaries. "And that can feel a bit strange . . . there's a hole in the story."[4] Hinton and others in the field fill that hole with sound made primarily by their own bodies moving various objects gathered in a recording studio. For the spider, Hinton used a Slinky to make sounds for the images of spinning a web, and then tapped his fingers on a reel of recording tape for the animal's movement along it.

Lifting the curtain on foley is very much like lifting the curtain on the Wizard of Oz—who is in fact engaged in foley, adding sounds of thunder to accompany flashes of flame, when Dorothy's dog Toto reveals that he is not a wizard but "a humbug." A humbug perhaps, but a very creative one, filling a hole in the story and successfully carrying it forward. As Hinton says, "I really like doing stuff like this, because I get carte blanche to be a little creative. Because there's no perceivable sound in nature, it means I can kind of make something up."

Give a foley artist footage of a tree falling in a forest, and they will give you the sound no one is there to hear.

We might be quick to acknowledge the labor of foley artists because it depends on the work of a human body. Even in the digital era, foley has remained very physical labor, largely unchanged since Jack Foley's time—people in sandboxes stamping with different-weight shoes.

Consider the irony if we do not also acknowledge the labor of capturing real sounds in nature through field recording. If, that is, like Spotify, we take it for granted that the sound of one wave is the same as any other, disconnected from human labor—unless it's made not by the ocean but by a person like Richard Hinton, sloshing a fistful of discarded recording tape through a tub of water in a studio.

The ubiquity of recording tape in foley is emblematic of this contradiction. Used for its primary function—recording sound—tape can become an object divorced from our labor, with a value potentially reduced to zero. Used off-label, as it were, as a crinkly, squeaky, crushable, tappable, flappable roll of plastic in the foley studio, it is transformed into a tool for readily acknowledged human work. Work that always has value.

Poet Charles Bernstein has written, "A piece of paper with nothing on it has a definite economic value. If you print a poem on it, this value is lost."[5] The cultural capital of sound in the U.S. is perhaps not as low as that of poetry—yet. But the witticism might still apply, at least for this example: in the digital era, audio tape can be worth more to nature documentarians as a tool for foley than as a medium for field recording.

Another reason nature documentarians turn to foley is to isolate sounds. In natural settings, any sound inevitably comes fused with other sounds. The composer and environmentalist R. Murray Schafer coined the term *soundscape* in the 1970s to express the breadth and depth of natural sound: "My approach . . . has been to treat the world soundscape as a huge macrocosmic composition," he wrote in "The Music of the Environment" (1973), comparing it to a symphony.[6] The orchestral analogy is deliberate: natural sounds come en masse. Even if we are temporarily focused on a soloist, there are innumerable aspects to the larger sonic setting that cannot—or Schafer might say *must not*—be ignored.

Schafer's view of the soundscape as music is more than an analogy; it is consistent with modernist ideas about music, accelerated with the introduction of electronic tools, that dissolved traditional instrumental sounds and tropes into abstract components. In the early part of the twentieth century, Edgard Varèse proposed a redefinition of music itself as *organized sound*. "As far back as the 1920s, I decided to call my music 'organized sound' and myself, not a musician, but 'a worker in rhythms, frequencies, and intensities,' " wrote Varèse in 1962, explaining the ease with which he could adopt the new electronic music tools of his day.[7] Varèse along with many experimental composers came to see orchestral sounds as a special case among infinite possibilities of combining fundamental variables—variables that synthesizers could translate to dials and switches and rearrange at will.

Once all sounds can be considered part of music, it's a short step to finding music in the soundscape at large, as Schafer did. The only missing ingredient is the composer—the organizer of sound, in Varèse's terminology. We might also see that missing bit as the human labor transforming a natural resource—sound—into value. Organizing sound is an act of labor, whether on paper like a traditional Western composer, or on tape like an electronic musician or field recordist. Note Varèse's description of his role as "a *worker* in rhythms, frequencies, and intensities."

Perhaps it is no coincidence, then, that two of the most widely regarded recordists of natural soundscapes, Bernie Krause and Chris Watson, started their careers in electronic music. In the mid-1960s, Bernie Krause was a session guitarist in Los Angeles when he got hold of an early Moog synthesizer, the first one on the West Coast. He and his musical partner Paul Beaver started demonstrating this confusing new tool to other artists, earning a

Sound Has Value 43

percentage from Moog on any resulting sales. Krause then found himself called into the studio to operate the machine when the artists he had sold it to couldn't figure it out. He ended up working with the Doors, the Byrds, George Harrison, and a host of other 1960s musicians, as well as on soundtracks for dozens of Hollywood movies including *Rosemary's Baby* and *Love Story*. But Krause says the day he wandered into a public park with a microphone to capture some natural sounds for an ecologically themed album (*In a Wild Sanctuary*, 1970), he realized what he wanted to listen to and record the rest of his life. After completing work on the soundtrack to *Apocalypse Now* (1979)—Krause is responsible for those indelible helicopter sounds, created on a Moog—he quit the studio and has been in the field ever since.

Chris Watson, the prolific U.K. recordist, started out in the post-punk band Cabaret Voltaire. Watson, too, was drawn to experimental electronic sounds, building his own modular synths and using tape manipulation to stamp early Cabaret Voltaire work with an unmistakable sonic signature. Right around the time Krause was turning his back on Hollywood, Watson had a revelation that led to his quitting Cabaret Voltaire and similarly shifting careers.

"Ian [Curtis] from Joy Division died, which had a strong effect on us all, and a couple other friends fell by wayside like that," he told *Electronic Sound* magazine in 2021, some forty years after the events. "If there was one moment that made me decide, it was probably when we went to the 'Top of the Pops' studio with New Order. I think Soft Cell were at Number One with 'Tainted Love,' and New Order were booked to appear on the show. . . .

And I looked around and thought, 'This is the last place on earth I ever want to be'—the environment, I mean, not the friends who'd invited us down. I thought, 'This is really shit. I'd rather be outside at night with a microphone, recording in a wood somewhere.'"[8] Which is exactly where he headed instead.

Tellingly, Watson describes the *environment* of "Top of the Pops" as what he wanted to escape in 1981, not his friends and not necessarily the music they were making together. Similarly, Krause credits the pursuit of a beneficial environment with the direction he chose for his second career. "I have a personal confession to make," he said in an interview conducted for the catalogue to his sound installation *The Great Animal Orchestra* (2016). "The main reason I have pursued this art and craft in the field of soundscape ecology is because being present in what remains of the wild natural environments simply makes me feel more alive, alert, and conscious of the wonders of life around me."[9]

This might seem like a return to the value of sound in terms of human health. But Watson and Krause both have a wider view of the value of soundscape than its salutary effect on the spirit. The two are engaged in what is truly an ecological crusade to value the sounds of the earth—both geophony and biophony—for their own sake. And both are documenting information about the damage humans are doing to the environment. Bernie Krause now estimates that half of his archived recordings "are from habitats that no longer exist, are radically altered because of human endeavor, or have gone altogether silent."[10] Krause is very clear in his writings and statements that he believes there is an urgency to the information he documents:

Sound Has Value

In the end—before the forest and marine echoes die—we may want to listen carefully to these biophonies, the essentials we cannot see or touch. They will tell us that we are not separate, but a vital part of one fragile biological place. How many of us will grasp the lesson in time?[11]

Chris Watson is less eager to foreground the crusading aspect of his work, although he works tirelessly to share it via radio, podcast, exhibition, and performance. As he told interviewer Luke Turner for online magazine the Quietus in 2013,

> I'm aware that there's a wider political aspect to my work but it's not my job to lecture. People need to decide for themselves. The better informed you are then you can start to realize what's happening. If the plants go, it will be a silent world, so there is a message in that. But I'm not a scientist so I don't lecture, but I am well aware that the more you know about something, the more likely you are to be concerned about it, and to do something about it.[12]

There is a punk-rock ethos in Chris Watson's approach: people need to do it themselves—share the information, and they will take it from there. "Sound is strong and visceral and strikes directly into our hearts and imaginations," he told *Electronic Sound*. "People just get it."[13]

Watson's and Krause's long labors of recording soundscapes in the field may have less commercial value than the foley produced for nature documentaries—"natural" sound work they are both also familiar with, and have participated in. Nonetheless, the value of their labor is clear. What they have each recorded is irreplaceable—literally, because so much of it has been lost to climate change and biological extinction. But it is also unreproducible because it is the work of individuals. That the subject matter of their documentation is nature changes nothing of the labor invested in it, even if we can't tell one wave from the next.

. . . Although perhaps Chris Watson can, as he recounted to Matthew Blackwell for the newsletter Tone Glow. It seems Watson once casually remarked to David Attenborough that "the sound of Pacific surf is something I really enjoy. It's really rich harmonically, and it has a musicality to it and it's not particularly loud, but it really has this deep, sort of life-affirming quality to it, a richness to it." Attenborough challenged him in response: " 'What, do you mean to tell me that you can tell the difference between different oceans?' "[14]

Watson's answer was unequivocally, "Yes!"—so he set out to demonstrate the difference for his long-standing work partner.

> I ended up making him a CD (laughs), a one-off CD to compare and contrast the sound of these two oceans. I could certainly hear the difference . . . and not necessarily just the Pacific or just the Atlantic, but there's certainly a lot of variety and similarity in the sounds of waves, which are basically bubbles bursting, wherever they are, due to the dynamics and the temperature conditions and weather conditions. So that's where that came from, and it's sort of grown a bit out of that, out of this conversation I had with David in a bar (laughs). It's now become sort of world-wide public knowledge (laughter). He's still got the CD, actually, I asked him about it.

Would that be a CD of no intrinsic value, with sounds of waves like any other? Or a precious artifact created by the specialized labor of a singular recordist.

5 backstage

Backstage used to be a very social space. Bored or anxious, hungry or high, wired or exhausted, musicians waited around with little to do but talk. That talk could turn paranoid—in the eighties, I heard *a lot* about UFOs—or comic, or nasty. Drummer Charlie Watts famously said in 1986 that being in the Rolling Stones had been "work five years and twenty years hanging around."

Today, backstages can be silent. People are on their smartphones or laptops and wearing headphones—not so different from an office, really. And like an office, it's productive. There are social media accounts to tend, emails to answer, day jobs to hold down remotely. Who has time to waste talking about UFOs?

Digital tools have made us more productive by occupying all our time, and musicians are no exception. But time, to borrow the language of business, is a zero-sum game. Every productive minute is a minute lost to hanging out. A future Charlie Watts might end up with five years behind the drums and twenty years on a laptop. But had Charlie Watts spent twenty out of twenty-five years on a laptop, you might say that he'd been an office worker with a part-time job in music. Which is precisely what is happening to many professional musicians today.

What's being eliminated is the "unproductive" time of being a musician. As anthropologists well know, actions that might look unproductive to an outside observer can have important if not crucial functions for a culture. Hanging around, for musicians, isn't empty time—it's time filled with exchange of information and social interactions. It's time spent building and maintaining a community, in other words.

Building and maintaining a community takes work. It too is a form of labor. It may not be the type of labor our economy rewards, but that does not alter its function; it only fails to acknowledge and encourage its achievements.

If you're not a musician and cannot imagine how hanging out backstage or in a van or studio could be part of professional activity, consider the distinction that media scholar Walter Ong draws between "oral" and "literate" cultures. Ong proposes that aspects of "primary orality" can persist in subcultures of literate societies:

> Today primary oral culture in the strict sense hardly exists, since every culture knows of writing and has some experience of its effects. Still, to varying degrees many cultures and subcultures, even

in a high-technology ambiance, preserve much of the mindset of primary orality.

Working in music before digital communications could well be described in terms of oral culture. Music—in particular, nonwritten music—shares much with Ong's descriptions of language in a primary oral culture. Ong was a Jesuit priest as well as a literary scholar, and he describes the role of sound in language with almost mystical overtones, assigning it properties outside our usual understanding of space and time.

> Without writing, words as such have no visual presence, even when the objects they represent are visual. They are sounds. You might "call" them back—"recall" them. But there is nowhere to "look" for them. They have no focus and no trace . . . not even a trajectory. They are occurrences, events. . . . All sensation takes place in time, but sound has a special relationship to time. . . . Sound exists only when it is going out of existence. It is not simply perishable but essentially evanescent. . . . There is no way to stop sound and have sound. I can stop a moving picture camera and hold one frame fixed on the screen. If I stop the movement of sound, I have nothing—only silence, no sound at all.[1]

We can't freeze sound. We can't see it. And this, to Ong, is precisely how oral cultures treat words and why the technological shift to writing represents such a fundamental change in human and social psychology. In sacred terms—always the background to Ong's thoughts—literacy transforms "the Word" into "the Book," mapping the power of sound onto an object.

Digital technology has brought a similar change to nonwritten music in the past few decades, I believe. The invention of recording in the early twentieth century made sound plastic, something we could hold and shape. But only in the digital era did sound became something we routinely *see*. Today, in the recording studio, we look at sound constantly on a screen. Now we can freeze it, not just stop it, as on vinyl or tape, but freeze it, like a single frame of film as Ong describes. In these infinitesimally small frames—their detail limited only by the resolution of our files and the processing power of our computers—we do not find silence but micro-moments of sound. They may be too quick for our ears but nonetheless they are clearly, resolutely there for us to see in time and space. Their evanescence, as Ong puts it, has been sacrificed for a new technology.

Ong assigns a set of practices to oral culture that mirror my experience of hanging out in pre-smartphone dressing rooms and tour vans, including "its participatory mystique, its fostering of a communal sense, its concentration on the present moment, and . . . its use of formulas."[2] Each of these shows up in clichés about musicians—if you've never been in a band with its participatory mystique and concentration on the present moment, watch *This Is Spinal Tap*. And if you want to watch the film like a musician, play it over and over till you've memorized its gags and turned them into formulas. (*Spinal Tap* was a flop in its theatrical release, but bands kept it on a loop in tour buses till it reemerged as a cult classic.) As my jazz-singer mother, Nancy Harrow, sometimes complains, "Musicians tell the same stories over and over." But like the parables and maxims of traditional cultures, those repeated anecdotes traded in the van and backstage form a web of shared information—crucial for a community based on orality.

I suppose I was raised to hang out with musicians, after a fashion. I loved the company of my mother's musician friends from as far back as I can remember. The first time I ever said my own name was caught by one of her rehearsal tapes made in our apartment—with Herbie Hancock as a witness, no less. He was a young pianist then, working as an accompanist for my mom, and there must have been no other childcare available so I became part of the rehearsal. "Damon," a small voice says on the tape, between takes. "Did you hear that?!" says an excited Herbie Hancock. "He said his name! Say it again! Say it again!" "Damon," the small voice obliges.

Many decades later, Herbie was at Harvard to deliver the prestigious Norton Lectures. Afterward, I walked to the lip of the stage in the grand hall with other well-wishers. He spotted me two or three deep in the crowd, did a double take, and suddenly said, "Damon? Did you know the first time you said your name . . ."

I was amazed he could recognize me; I hadn't seen him face to face since I was a teenager (though I know I've come to resemble both my parents). And I was delighted to find my own family lore had become a proper musician's anecdote, ready for repetition.

When I was a little bit older than that voice on the rehearsal tape, the trombonist Bob Brookmeyer and songwriter Margo Guryan (who were married at the time) used to mind me for my parents—neither had kids of their own then, and they seemed to enjoy sitting in, as it were. Bob was impossibly tall, liked to play touch football, and made me laugh just as hard as he did the adults (although with different techniques: his conversation was so full of slang and quick asides it wasn't till adolescence that I could start to pick up on his verbal jokes). A few years after that, when I no longer needed a babysitter, I would be doing homework while my parents played bridge with their pianist friends John and Mirjana Lewis, often with the latest Modern Jazz Quartet test pressing on the stereo. John would hum to himself as he listened and sorted his hand, just as I saw him do at the piano in performance. The four of them would talk late into the night over cards and cognac—I know they kept score, but the game never seemed too important.

Other evenings at my parents' house with their musician friends were more raucous, especially when Bertram Ross the dancer and his partner the cabaret songwriter John Wallowitch came over. Bert was a master of Jewish humor, telling classic jokes in various outrageous accents and attitudes. And John would inevitably end up at the piano, singing ribald lyrics or viciously mimicking some performer he didn't like. Later the two had a cabaret act together, and it was not so different from the performances I had grown up witnessing in our apartment, although I could no longer retreat to my bedroom when John started to get maudlin.

My mother asked a number of her friends to teach me different instruments—piano, guitar, drums. I was never much for reading music, so formal lessons would invariably slow and eventually stop. But once I began playing music in bands of my own, the hanging out part came easy. I didn't know the ins and outs of gigging, recording, or trying to keep a group together—those were all lessons I learned the hard way, as they came. And I'm still not good at reading charts. But talking into the night, the silly jokes, the repeated stories, even the maudlin moments were all right there, same as I knew from childhood. This was a culture whose folkways I had long ago absorbed. The lessons were received, after all.

It seems more than coincidence to me that as musicians lose the orality of our subculture, we are also losing societal acknowledgment of and fair pay for our labor. Because measured in literate terms—in metrics that the office world recognizes, of emails and spreadsheets and Slack channels—what did Charlie Watts do all those years he wasn't onstage? It takes a different idea of labor to appreciate everything he did that went into the perfect backbeat.

6 music is labor

Sound is a material, a part of the environment; it has value, and that value can be determined by labor. Music, a valuable use of sound by any human measure, is an example of that labor.

And yet as a musician, I've been asked innumerable times: Yes, but what do you do for *work?*

It's not unreasonable, given the precarious state of affairs for arts in the digital era, to wonder how a musician or any artist manages to make a living. Still, that's not the question usually posed, or at least not how it's framed. And maybe this is part of the reason why being a musician is such a precarious form of labor—because it's not recognized as such. In the United States, most musicians are barred from unionizing because we are not salaried workers. We receive no benefits from our employers, we have to pay our own health insurance and Social Security taxes, and as a result we often have to take multiple jobs. Many of those additional jobs are connected to music, yet don't seem to count as nonlabor in the same way, such as teaching, or working in a music store, record shop, or at a venue; as crew or tech on the road; at record companies, booking agencies, publishers, distributors; at streaming platforms . . .

Why does it seem as if only our work as musicians is dismissed as nonlabor? In my experience, even many musicians are quick to say that what they do is not labor—and looming large among their reasons is the allure of intellectual property.

Property is a word that smacks of bosses, not workers. According to the AFL-CIO, the average S&P 500 company's CEO-to-worker pay ratio in 2022 was 272 to 1. And of all those corporations, it was one in music, Live Nation, that had the worst ratio of all, with a median worker pay of $25,673 and a CEO earning 5,414 times that amount.[1]

That $25,673 median pay for a worker with Live Nation is not the salary of a property owner. It is in fact not a living wage, even for a single person without any dependents, in any state in the U.S.[2] In the United Kingdom, the Musicians Union completed the first ever census of musicians in 2023 and concluded that "of those making 100% of their income from music, the average annual income is around £30,000."[3] The "minimum income standard" in the U.K. for a single-person household with no dependents in 2023 was £29,500.[4]

Who can blame a struggling musician for jumping at the chance to own any property, even if it is only intellectual? But this opportunity is often presented as a trade—musicians aren't acknowledged as workers *because* we can generate and own intellectual property. Were we paid as work for hire instead, we would have no claim on the rights of what we create. And wouldn't you rather have rights over intellectual property than not?

But consider all the many rights musicians have surrendered by not being acknowledged as workers: the right to unionize; the right to demand a living wage; the right to health care; social security, disability, and unemployment insurance; safe workplaces—all the many protections won by the labor movement over the course of the long twentieth century. For the most part, working musicians in the U.S. don't enjoy any of these rights or benefits unless they hold one of the few salaried positions remaining with an orchestra or in a Broadway pit. After more than thirty years as a working musician, I have never met anyone who has one of those jobs. There is a world of us out here with lots of intellectual property and no workers' rights.

Whether we maintain effective rights over our intellectual property is another slippery question. There's a concept in European law that is more or less foreign to the U.S. legal system, called "the moral right of the artist." The idea is that there are certain aspects of copyright which cannot be signed away—they attach to the work and its creator regardless of contracts. In the U.S., copyright is seen as an economic issue only. Like any other aspect of property, it can be sold, reassigned, or given away. Intellectual property is, in this regard, nothing special. But for the artist, it can seem like the only accessible source of power and wealth—it is property, after all. And it's conjured out of nothing but ideas.

This endless fount of property is like the original sin of art in America. When you start to create, you start to generate property. Exciting, no? But it is also, in my experience starting from the very beginning of my career in recorded music, problematic. The first thing my youthful band Galaxie 500 did—aside from being friends, forming a band, and starting to write songs together— was negotiate intellectual property rights. We signed a homemade "contract" with an equally young guy in Boston to put out our first single. This was going to pay for his grandchildren's braces, he said, with a strange gleam in his eyes. And then, after the initial copies sold, he refused to repress the record because whatever copies he had saved for himself would be more valuable as collectors' items. Our first and at that point only recording was deliberately deleted almost as soon as it had been released. And we had no say in the matter.

What I learned this quickly was that we could lose our intellectual property rights simply by signing a piece of paper.

Of course the paper could have all kinds of clauses in it protecting our rights under various conditions. So the next contract we signed—with the same guy! (fool me twice, shame on me)— gave away our debut album, but this time with language assuring that it would come back to us if . . . and if . . . and if . . .

The next lesson I learned was that proving a protective clause in a contract has been triggered often requires hiring a lawyer. And lawyers, as everyone knows, cost money. Effectively, our protections on paper were only as good as the lawyer we could afford to enforce them. We had signed away our intellectual property and needed cash to get it back.

How to get that cash? For my young band, as for so many others, it meant signing another contract with a bigger label, and with many more clauses in it.

I probably don't need to spell out what often happens next. In our particular case, it took this form: when the bigger label that gave you an advance with which you paid a lawyer to rescue you from your prior contract *later declares bankruptcy,* you're going to need another lawyer (music lawyers don't do bankruptcy) to try and get your rights back from the auction held to liquidate that label's assets, *which now include your intellectual property.*

I felt much older but was still in my twenties when I went into that bankruptcy auction with nothing but amateur documents I prepared myself (Galaxie 500 had since broken up, so there was no yet-bigger advance to pay for yet another lawyer to get us out of this fresh mess). My goal was to extricate our intellectual property and return it to our collective possession. I'm happy to report that we won. But what it took was renouncing all the royalties we were owed from our recording contracts to that date. Which meant that any money we earned while Galaxie 500 was a working band did not come from our intellectual property, because we had in fact never received any of the royalties promised by any of our original recording contracts.

Yet we had earned money—a living, even—while in that band. What from?

Now we're on the scent of the real thing, no red herring of intellectual property transferred by a signature dragged across paper. Because if you follow the money we actually earned while in Galaxie 500, I believe we were paid for our labor. For our labor at shows, collected at the end of each night (usually in cash). And for our labor writing and recording songs, paid out of a budget provided by the record company for us to complete that work.

There's nothing about intellectual property in those exchanges. Do this, get paid X for it. Have someone else do work for you, pay them X for it. These are the same as payments for labor in any job.

So why all the hullabaloo around those contracts we signed, which ended up negated anyway? We had been told it was our intellectual property that gave us earning power in music. But in fact, it seems we had been selling our labor all along.

In the U.S., you cannot sign away your labor, legally; that's indentured servitude. But you *can* sign away your intellectual property. That's the music business.

As I write this, there is a lot of hand-wringing about artificial intelligence (AI) and its potential effect on the music industry. This issue might seem to have come up all of a sudden, although of course the technology has been long in the works. Those in the vanguard, like the artist Holly Herndon, have gotten ahead of the crowd and already thought hard about how to use these new tools creatively, and (as she hopes) positively for the community. But constructive use of AI won't prevent its commercial or financial abuse, which is what most of the present hand-wringing is about.

Many artists are turning to the protection of intellectual property as a strategy to preserve their interests in this new world of machine learning. An impressive number of music advocacy organizations came together as the Human Artistry Campaign and proposed a seven-point "Core Principles for Artificial Intelligence Applications in Support of Human Creativity and Accomplishment."[5] Most of those points focus on copyright—restricting it to "human creativity" and thus denying it to works made by AI.

But copyright is just a legal tool. And while it may be intended to protect individual creative labor—as those reaching for it in the potential fight against AI are hoping—it is a more powerful tool in the hands of those with capital than it is in the hands of artists without such resources. In that regard, I would assert, it has already failed most working musicians.

Take two twentieth-century legal cases that would seem to form a precedent for the protection of artists from vocal imitation. Holly Herndon cites them in a discussion of existing Voice Model Rights on her website introducing the remarkable AI-based Voice Tool she developed, Holly+.[6] One is *Bette Midler v. Ford Motor Company;* the other is *Tom Waits v. Frito-Lay.* In both, an artist brought suit against a corporation for imitating their voice without compensation, and in both cases the artist won. These judgments should be a legal bulwark against the wanton use of vocal models by AI—one of the potential uses of this technology that most concerns musicians.

Now consider a common experience that many of my fellow musicians and I have had well before the advent of AI. An offer comes in for commercial use of one of our songs. We ask our representatives if we might get more for that use. And we are cautioned, Maybe, but don't ask for too much because then they might just copy your work instead of paying you anything at all.

Which is precisely what happened to Bette Midler and Tom Waits. But they had resources to sue in response, and most of us don't.

In other words, copyright isn't effective protection on its own for artists. If you don't have the capital to go to court against corporations like Ford and Frito-Lay, you have to assume they will copy your work if they so choose. Which leaves artists to negotiate from a position of weakness for use of their work, regardless of copyright ownership. Is that so different from what we now face with AI, which has been developed by some of the largest corporations in the world, like Microsoft and Google?

What working artists need is to address the power imbalance between corporations and creators. Individual creative artists are at a tremendous disadvantage in power struggles over AI, or any other technology developed and used by massively capitalized corporations. Copyright protections cannot correct that imbalance. However, organized labor can. We know it can because it has before.

This is an old answer to what might seem like a new problem. But the problem creators face from AI is not as new as the technology. It's as old as capitalism, and as out of control as we have let it become in the twenty-first century.

As we have seen, sound is a material, it's a material with value, and in other situations that value can be determined by labor. So why not with music, too? Why not reframe the economic problems faced by musicians and view them as a question of fair pay for labor, rather than a question of intellectual property rights. I am not advocating for the elimination of copyright; it has a crucial role to play for creators in many situations. But my experience as a musician tells me not to count on it for making a living. My work is labor like anyone else's and deserves the same protections.

There remains a problem for contemporary musicians willing to view their work as labor, however: What *is* labor in the digital economy?

Live performance is a relatively obvious and old-fashioned example of music as labor. For anyone who has ever been on tour, the labor involved certainly needs no explanation. But even if you have never lugged your instruments across state lines, time zones, and international borders, it is clear from the audience how much work is involved in getting onstage and playing a show. The sweat often shows.

Nevertheless, recently there has been an outbreak of strangely dismissive behavior toward performers onstage. For some reason audiences have started throwing things at pop stars, not in displeasure but not exactly in adulation either. Drake was hit by a cellphone. Harry Styles was hit by a vape pen, hard enough to double him over and send him offstage. Cardi B had a drink thrown at her (she threw the microphone back in retaliation). It's become frequent enough that Adele chose a preemptive strategy. "I fucking dare you," she told her crowd. "Dare you to throw something at me and I'll fucking kill you."

No one seems to understand why pop stars are being hit with projectiles, but what it calls to mind for me is the one-way interaction with music that we have become accustomed to online. It's as if these audience members don't realize they are now in an actual exchange with the performer. For many fans, the fourth wall has been largely replaced by a screen—which wouldn't be pierced by objects so much as repel them.

But I'm interested less in chasing ideas of digital passivity (often exaggerated, I believe) than of digital value. How could those in an audience not see their own contribution in the evolving exchange taking place at a live performance? Or might it be that they only see value in terms of the ticket price. They paid their money and then felt they could do as they liked—even if it meant injuring the performer—because that purchase is the sole value they could imagine contributing.

This mirrors the extractive relationship listeners have to online platforms that provide them with music. Digital music is free, if you want it, so long as you accept this structure to the exchange: the platform gets your time, attention, and personal data, and you get access to music. It's not even a purchase. It's more a mining operation, with the listener as object.

Passivity is cultivated by this relationship, to be sure. But there is enough room for directed action within these platforms to create fan armies, for example. What there isn't room for is any kind of value generated by actions of the user. All value goes to the platform. Once we submit to data extraction, our value is measured simply by time spent as a consumer.

Cut to the venue. Time at a show might seem analogous to time on a platform: you enter, you get access to music, eventually you leave. It might seem as if there is no value generated by your activities while there, apart from purchasing your ticket and perhaps add-ons like drinks and merch.

This could explain the complaints some indie rock artists have been making about audience behavior as well. Jack White is the latest to join a long list trying to ban smartphones from venues—a gesture that might be dismissed as curmudgeonly from an analog-loving revivalist. But Mitski, who doesn't fetishize the 1920s like Jack White, also recently complained about people filming her shows rather than experiencing them. "When I'm on stage and look to you but you are gazing into a screen, it makes me feel as though those of us on stage are being taken from and consumed as content, instead of getting to share a moment with you," she wrote on social media in a now-deleted series of posts.[7] Adrianne Lenker of Big Thief posted a video explaining to fans that "when music is happening in a room, there's a performer onstage playing and doing their craft; when you enter into that space, try to be mindful of what's happening and pay attention."[8]

Pay attention . . . even the language we use for this activity engages the concept of value. The audience has more to contribute to a performance than simply entering the space—and they have more to pay than the price of a ticket.

Social media and streaming platforms know this very well. Indeed, the value of attention is so great for platforms that they have largely done away with the equivalent of ticket price altogether and made access to music free. But they then strip the audience of the value of their own attention.

If the value of our engagement online is attention, and that value is wholly taken from us by the platforms that profit from it, it follows that at present we are alienated from our attention in the same manner that workers are alienated from their labor in an industrial economy. It's a quick jump from not feeling you own the value of your attention to not feeling like a participant in an exchange of attention with the performer.

But what precisely is the value of attention when it's not in an extractive relationship that uses data collection to convert it to cash? How does one even identify attention in a physical environment like performance?

Musicians know the value of attention viscerally. Nonetheless, it is rather mysterious and difficult to describe. In Adrianne Lenker's video message to fans, the singer lit a candle and resorted to talk about "magic" in an effort to convey what attention does for a room. This isn't the usual way we discuss value. Attention can be felt, but not with fingertips. And certainly not like a cellphone or vape pen thrown at one's head.

So where and how to locate that value of attention? Karl Marx had, I believe, a similar quandary in locating the value of any labor. "Labor is creative of value," wrote the philosopher Jacques Rancière in a gloss on Marx's *Capital*. "*It does not have value.*"[9] The "labor theory of value"—the idea that value is a kind of repository of labor—is often wrongly ascribed to Marx, who made extensive use of this classical economic concept from Adam Smith and David Ricardo, but primarily to critique it. The "value theory of labor" is one clever way to identify what Marx was really after, in a memorable phrase coined by the British economist Diane Elson—which, if I understand it correctly, expresses the idea that *value determines the nature of labor* in a capitalist economy, rather than the other way around.[10]

If we apply Elson's formula to our post-industrial online economy, where attention is the creator of value . . . then isn't our attention, in effect, our digital labor?

That is to say, attention has value online, but not only online. The performance space makes this clear. And if attention has value, then crucially its value is not created by its digital extractors. It is created by us, and therefore belongs to us. It too is a form of human labor.

Attention as a form of labor offers a way to understand the labor of sound in general, and music in particular. It is attention that field recordists bring to the soundscapes they document. It is a lack of attention that allows noise to accumulate in the environment like so much waste. And for working musicians, attention to sound is what directs our engagement with our instruments, with other musicians, with recording, and with the audience. We shape sounds for a living.

At least, we try to make a living at it.

If we have online platforms to thank for isolating attention as a source of value in the digital economy, we also have them to blame for robbing us of that value. This applies equally to the players and the consumers of music. Platforms are designed so that neither creator nor audience profits.

This theft of value from musicians' labor in the digital realm is a twenty-first-century version of the shell game we played in the twentieth century with intellectual property. We have come up empty-handed again. But this time, no one is winning. The platforms that dominate music streaming—Spotify, Apple, and Amazon—don't seem to be making a decent profit from music either. Spotify is by far the largest player in the industry, with twice the market share of its nearest competitors. Yet Spotify almost never shows a profit from music, reporting losses in quarterly report after quarterly report.

If the biggest player in the recorded music industry cannot make a profit, something must be wrong with the business model. Unless—like the fictional *Producers* aiming for a Broadway flop or the real-life financiers of the subprime mortgage crisis—the streaming business model isn't about the value of its ostensible product at all. Indeed, Spotify's financial success as a company seems to depend on the perception of music as valueless. In the Swedish academic study *Spotify Teardown* (2019), the authors describe how Spotify's founder, Daniel Ek, and his colleagues created their business by treating music like junk bonds, or overstock goods:

> When Daniel Ek, Martin Lorentzon, and others first developed Spotify, they famously did so by building on a collection of music they did not hold any rights to themselves. The history of music streaming thus begins with an act of free riding—or arbitrage. As arbitrageurs of music, Ek and his colleagues would obtain scarce goods at no cost, with the aim of making revenue through advertising and later subscriptions, while others involved in the transaction—the composers, musicians, music publishers, artists, and repertoire owners—experienced an implicit loss.[11]

Spotify used the financial model of arbitrage to obtain a cheap if not free product—digital music—and resell it in a new context to realize a profit. In other words, Spotify's profit requires that digital music have little to no value. Spotify executives continually talk down the value of music—they offer it for free; they tell musicians we are lucky to be paid anything for it; they insist that without their service there is only piracy and zero income. Most tellingly, they invest nothing back into music. Unlike a record label, publisher, or almost anyone else in the traditional music industry, Spotify devotes none of its revenue to the development of new recording artists.

Meanwhile, as it continues to lose money on music, Spotify amasses huge wealth—it is valued at tens of billions of dollars on the New York Stock Exchange, and its executives are among the highest paid in the entire music industry. But read investors' bulletins about the company, and you'll find they take for granted that Spotify may never turn a consistent profit from music. The question they ask instead is, Can the company redirect the money it draws out of music into a more profitable pursuit?

As for Spotify's competitors, Apple and Amazon, they have already found those more profitable pursuits—they could drop music tomorrow and not alter their extremely successful business models. They well might. After all, if streaming music is not making even the market leader a profit, where's the value in it?

The platform economy has devalued sound, but not only sound. Journalists, writers, photographers, filmmakers . . . everyone working in media has experienced a similar devaluation of work during the tech boom of the digital era. Musicians have in many ways had the dubious distinction of going first in this regard—the proverbial canaries in the coalmine. But we aren't silent yet.

7 at the merch table

As the value of recorded music has plummeted due to free or nearly free access via streaming platforms, many musicians have focused on live music for income. Performance itself is not the only source of income on tour, however; the other crucial component is merchandise. The merch table is for some a last meaningful outlet for physical sales of recorded music, not to mention branded T-shirts and tchotchkes. You might think these kinds of sales would all happen online today, where so much retail resides. But every musician knows that nothing online can rival the sales that take place in person at venues, from bar gigs to stadiums.

It's more than convenience that makes these physical sales happen, in other words. At venues people will wait their turn, limit themselves to choices immediately available, and carry goods home—everything Amazon has built a fortune by helping consumers avoid. There's something about being together with other fans of the same music, or even—if the venue is small enough—with the musicians themselves at the merch table that short-circuits those calculations. Were Amazon to replicate this experience online its owners would make even more for themselves. It can't.

What happens at the merch table isn't mysterious, it's simply what used to happen in every neighborhood store. People chat. Fans talk to the salesperson, or to the musicians if they're selling the goods themselves. They discuss their choices—How small is the Small shirt? Which album has the songs I heard tonight?—and they share their deliberations over a purchase. If you're on the road, people will often ask what you think of their city and then share local recommendations: foods you should try, places you should visit. Sometimes when I'm at the merch table, and I know this happens to musicians a lot, I get the chance to hear remarkably personal stories from people moved to share them. This is exchange of an entirely different sort than via cash or card.

These nonmonetary exchanges at the merch table are related to the hanging out musicians do backstage and in the van, in that they help build community. Talk may not be a necessary part of a purchase—that's what Amazon figured out. But it is necessary to community.

My favorite fishmonger, Courthouse Fish Market in East Cambridge—one of Cambridge's longest operating businesses, open since 1912—recently closed. It is a family business and everyone in the family who worked there is approaching retirement age; they put it up for sale, and there were no takers. I asked the two brothers I have been buying from almost every week for decades who else they recommended in the business. There's no one left doing what we do, said Joe. No one wants to do this work any more, said Eddy—possibly including himself in the statement. They weren't morose; they were smiling, if a bit ruefully. They've earned their retirement.

"Are we really going to have to buy our fish from Amazon?" Naomi sighed, when I told her the news. The Amazon-owned chain store Whole Foods is where most of our immediate neighbors pick up fish, even though we live by the ocean in a region famous for the quality of its seafood. The fishmonger nearest our home closed a couple of years ago. The next nearest closed a decade ago. But I never went to either anyway, because I always preferred crossing town for Courthouse Fish.

At Courthouse, I learned a lot about fish from Eddy and Joe (and Al, the eldest brother, who retired some years ago), but I also learned a lot about my community. Regular patrons included the older Portuguese residents of East Cambridge, whom Eddy and Joe spoke to in the language they'd learned from their parents. More recent Brazilian immigrants came, also speaking Portuguese, of course, and so did the wider Caribbean community, with its mix of Creole, Spanish, and English. On Saturdays there were groups of young men from Gulf states like Qatar and the United Arab Emirates, temporary residents studying or working here and rooming together while they did. I met Moroccans,

South Asians, Japanese—pretty much everyone from anywhere near the sea who had come to Boston and was now looking to buy ingredients needed for their home cooking. I watched what they all bought, and I asked them all for recipes.

Eddy and Joe knew their customers; they gently warned people if they seemed to be wandering away from their usual budget, and they pointed out what was good that day and wouldn't be too expensive. There was a handwritten sign that EBT cards were welcome. They rolled their eyes when certain difficult characters walked in the door, or after they left. They gossiped about the town, griped about the government, avoided explicit politics but dropped hints that they weren't too thrilled with everything liberal Cambridge generally takes for granted. Older ladies were teasingly flirted with, guys were dissed now and then, and the parade of Harvard- and MIT-connected professionals seemed to be judged largely on their knowledge of fish. They remembered names and jobs, asked after spouses and children. And this was just the retail part of the business—they were down at the pier buying fish in the morning, and their network of suppliers had to be equally if not even more extensive.

They taught me which fish to buy in which season—what was local, what was brought in from where, what was especially good right now, and what was unfortunately overpriced due to supply and demand. Whenever tuna hit prices they judged outrageous (the best tuna on the docks in Boston is auctioned to Japan and to New York restaurants), they didn't stock it at all, even though some customers would have bought it regardless. And when a quality fish fell to them at an especially good price, they put it out for less than you'd see anywhere else. They saved all the useful trimmings from large fish, selling heads and frames cheap for soup, and collars and bellies and roe to those of us who relish such things. (Their father ate roe for breakfast and consequently neither had developed a taste for it, they told me once as I gratefully took yet another pair off their hands.)

In time, I heard about their health, kids, holidays, family weddings, vacations (Eddy likes cruises), and eventually, although they didn't give much advance warning, plans for retirement. Their younger sister Diane runs the family fish restaurant next door, which has stayed open, so I can go in there and buy some things while they still supply and cut for her. The selection isn't what it was, but I'm grateful for it. Damned if I'll buy fish at Whole Foods if I can avoid it.

Regardless of the seafood I will or won't find for sale elsewhere, nothing will replace the role of Courthouse Fish in the community. The same happened when our local grocer shut, shortly before the pandemic. I used to see the kids from the neighborhood there after school buying candy at the register. And nannies from the big houses charging lamb chops to the family account. And older doctors and lawyers, sent for milk or eggs and picking up a box of cookies. And Peter Wolf (yes, that Peter Wolf, from the J. Geils Band), dressed in black from head to toe, putting his groceries in a paper bag. Where can I see them all now?

As neighborhood shops close, our neighborhoods becomes less visible to themselves. I will no longer meet as many in my community as I did at Courthouse Fish, or at our local grocer. Like everyone else I'll eventually go to one of the nearby chain supermarkets, use self-checkout to avoid the big lines at registers, and talk to no one while there.

A few days after Courthouse Fish closed, Condé Nast fired most of the staff at the music journalism website Pitchfork, including all its features editors, and folded what was left of it into the men's magazine *GQ*. I had a surprisingly similar feeling about this as I had about the closure of my neighborhood stores, even though a website with global reach like Pitchfork would seem to have more in common with Amazon than with a family business. But it is more than possible to build communities online—there are countless examples, starting with the beginnings of the internet as a way for individuals at physically scattered government and university locations to share mutually important information. Amazon is designed to make us consumers, not members of a community. And the loss of an online forum for writing about music is a blow to my very real colleagues in both journalism and music.

We cannot replace these spaces when we lose them, because their value is in the community that coalesced around them. Eddy and Joe couldn't find a buyer for their business because a neighborhood fish store—even one that's been in place for over a hundred years, with a devoted clientele—seems to be not of this era; it's a throwback. And so perhaps is a dedicated music journal, even a virtual one. Pitchfork had developed the strongest music journalism brand of its era, employed a series of superb editors and writers, and had a regular readership so large that according to one Condé Nast employee it was the most visited site in that media empire's entire portfolio. If not Pitchfork, with more daily visitors than *Vogue* or *Vanity Fair* or the *New Yorker*—or *GQ*—then who in music journalism can thrive in this economic environment?

And if no one can, then all we'll have left will be streaming platforms, their algorithms, and the atomized consumer behavior they push on us. A self-checkout counter for music, with a scanner going beep—beep—beep.

8 a community theory of value

Sound is a material of value whose worth can be measured by the labor of individuals, including musicians. In the digital realm, an aspect of that labor is shared by creator and audience alike: attention. It is attention that is monetized by digital platforms. And our attention is alienated by them, as labor is alienated by industrial capital. Online platforms that trade in attention—including Facebook/Meta, Google/Alphabet, and music streaming platforms such as Spotify, Apple, and Amazon—enrich themselves by realizing surplus value in attention, just as industrial capital depends and enriches itself on surplus labor.

Still, attention functions quite differently from labor in our economic lives. Labor can be measured at an individual level—an individual's labor is valued today in the same manner as during the heyday of industrial capitalism. However, an individual's attention in the digital era has no economic value. Whether I stream a given song or film, or click on a given article, means nothing in real terms. Only "at scale"—in the aggregate—can attention be monetized. Yet then it can be monetized to such a degree that some of the richest corporations in the world are powered by it.

It seems counterintuitive that valueless individual transactions can sum to great wealth, a mystery of the vaporous internet. But this is also something we experience viscerally every day in our cities and towns, where individual purchases no longer shape the economic landscape as before. This is especially true for media—including in my chosen professions, books and music.

I took a walk through my neighborhood, Harvard Square in Cambridge, and tried to remember the locations of all the bookstores there I used to visit. I counted sixteen. Two are now banks, one is a real estate company, two are in buildings since torn down, three are vacant and available for lease, three have been repurposed as offices by Harvard University, one is a Blue Bottle Coffee (owned by Nestlé), one sells jewelry, one cookies, one frozen yogurt, and one lingerie.

I know I am forgetting others—the *Harvard Crimson* reported that there were twenty-seven the year I graduated college, 1985, and in 1989 the *New York Times* visited Cambridge and counted "25 to 30."[1]

There are still five bookstores in operation—kudos to Harvard Book Store (general independent), the Grolier (poetry), Raven (used books), Million Year Picnic (graphic novels), and I suppose the Harvard Coop, although it is now run by the chain store Barnes & Noble, which is a Pyrrhic version of survival. But even those five seem awful lonely, given the ghosts of bookstores past I see in the streets around them.

What happened? Amazon, obviously, and the internet more generally. However, I believe there's a more precise way to identify this change, rather than through an account of digital-era winners and losers. The more fundamental change has been a shift in scale.

The storefronts that bookstores occupy, or used to, are human-sized spaces for selling hand-sized objects. In a university town like Cambridge, many of us would walk to them, especially in the evening (most were open late, because what else was there to do back in the twentieth century?), spend an inordinate amount of time standing around in them browsing, and leave with maybe a single item. One by one by one, books left their shops and entered our dorm rooms, apartments, houses, basements, and attics. What a painstaking, laborious process. We were building pyramids out of paper and ink.

Contrast this with the tech startup concept of "at scale," "to scale," or simply, "scale." In the context of online business, all uses of the word imply a massive scale which can no longer be measured by individuals. Margins may be minimal, or even nonexistent, as they were for years in Amazon's case. But if the scale is large enough, and the market thereby concentrated enough, untold riches follow.

I can repeat this same exercise in my neighborhood with record stores—I count fifteen in Harvard Square that I used to visit, but, again, I know I'm forgetting others. In this case, two are now banks, one is a cellphone store, one a real estate company, four are restaurants, one is a greeting card store, one a nail salon, two have been repurposed into offices, and three are still in business, one for new records (Newbury Comics, a local mini-chain that survives in part by selling non-music youth culture products) and two for used.

Spotify, like Amazon, works with tiny margins. Indeed, the company almost always claims a loss on its use of music. Yet like Amazon, Spotify monetizes this "loss" as part of a strategy for building dominant market share and thereby accumulating wealth via capital markets and business-to-business transactions. Despite the red ink it reports, the surplus that Spotify is amassing reveals itself whenever the owners feel like a showy splurge: on staggeringly expensive office space in New York ($2.77 million a month); on sponsorship of Barcelona's football club and stadium ($100 million a year); on lavish podcast contracts with celebrities like Prince Harry and Meghan Markle ($20 million), the Obamas ($25 million), or shock jock Joe Rogan ($200 million).[2]

Consider the scale of that last example: Joe Rogan's $200 million podcast deal with Spotify would require 66.666 billion streams to earn back at the average payout received by musicians from the platform ($0.003 per stream). This is equivalent to every person on the planet listening to the same song more than eight times.

That is not a scale based on numbers of people; if anything it's numbers of planets. To my non-algorithmic mind, the 66 billion streams that Joe Rogan's contract represents are simply uncountable. I understand that a computer counts differently from humans. But that's precisely the point. Businesses like Amazon and Spotify are designed for a nonhuman scale.

Nonhuman scale erases value from individual consumption and makes even modest small businesses based on those exchanges difficult to maintain. The resulting crisis in music is the same as in other media, including journalism (Harvard Square used to have two landmark newsstands at its center; one is now a tourist information center and the other a pizza parlor) and film (the two commercial theaters in Harvard Square have both closed; one is now the site of a future luxury mall and the other a yoga studio and vegetarian restaurant).

Fortunately, for film in Harvard Square we still have the historic Brattle Theatre, which—like Club Passim, survivor from another era of live music—is now a nonprofit. Also the grandest nonprofit of them all, Harvard University, with its $50 billion endowment, maintains the cinematheque Harvard Film Archive as part of its library system.

In a functioning town, shops provide services that are scaled to the community around them. But a functioning online business seeks a scale beyond community. If the two compete, the scale of online business affords it tools that have always been available to larger capital: lower margins, greater selection, more marketing, and so on. For a service that can be provided by online corporations, it's as if an invisible chain store has moved into the center of every small town and forced all local competition out of business. These chain stores are so big they can literally claim to be "Earth's Biggest Bookstore," or the equivalent in whatever business a given platform has managed to monopolize.

A Community Theory of Value 85

And yet—as our nonprofit arthouse cinemas attest—online businesses cannot provide everything that a community wants and needs. Individuals might be satisfied with the convenience and low price of streaming films at home. But the community, as a collective, goes wanting.

Philanthropy is one way that superannuated forms of exchange can persist. So is collectability—scarcity that raises prices to make up for a reduced audience. But neither of these strategies replicates the middle-class scale of individual exchange that supports the economic life of a city or town. Nonprofits generally depend on large donations from sources of great means, whether private individuals or foundations or government grants. Similarly, collectability generally aims at fewer, expensive purchases instead of many smaller, cheaper ones. There's a reason why antique stores and art galleries aren't a typical town center's mainstay. Of a resort town, yes—a place where people go on occasion and spend an unusual amount of money while there. But that's not a formula for the health of an economically mixed community, as Cambridge was when I first moved to it in the 1980s.

The nonprofit model is available to businesses that can establish noncommercial import to the wealthy or powerful. But philanthropists have yet to support small grocers and pharmacies, much less local banks and insurance companies. There are many businesses scaled to a community that a town needs to thrive. Harvard Square, to continue this examination of my own locale, has in the digital age lost the ability to serve its surrounding community's daily needs. We no longer have a hardware store, for example—although we now have storefronts representing every national phone service company.

The value of music can be framed in nonmonetary terms if you are filing a grant application for philanthropic support. But music also has economic value—and not only at scale, as a streaming corporation calculates it. Music on a human scale has value for a community. The music scholar Christopher Small coined a verb, *musicking,* to express the manner in which music is an activity as much as or even more than it is a noun. To Small, music is not an object of production and consumption so much as a model of community. He saw this most clearly in performance:

> When we perform, we bring into existence, for the duration of the performance, a set of relationships, between the sounds and between the participants, that model ideal relationships as we imagine them to be and allow us to learn about them by experiencing them.

Small identifies both the players and the audience as participants in musicking—and therefore sees this modeling of relationships through music as "reciprocal."

> In exploring we learn, from the sounds and from one another, the nature of the relationships; in affirming we teach one another about the relationships; and in celebrating we bring together the teaching and the learning in an act of social solidarity. The simultaneous inward and outward flow of information that goes on throughout the performance is made possible by the fact that the language of the information is not of words but of gestures.[3]

Listening is a crucial aspect of performance; it is an action as significant to the communicative process Small describes as the music itself. *Gestures,* emphasizes Small, are the basis of information exchange in musicking—and a gesture is not something there is much reason to do on your own. It is a means of communicating with others.

Coming from a classical music background, Small focused on performance in his analysis of musicking to distinguish that activity from the written score. For me, born in the golden age of analog recording and surrounded by genres of largely unwritten music like jazz and rock, the role of a score is not nearly as significant. However, I find Small's analysis of performance easily extended to recorded sound. Musical gestures—musicking—are legible through recordings, at least to my ears. A John Coltrane record *is* a performance. So is a Beach Boys multitrack construction. These albums include not only the gestures of the musicians but of the sound recordists, mastering engineers, vinyl cutters, designers of the artwork . . . Indeed, all the labor involved in a recording is legible as gesture if we listen for it. And as Small explains, it is that act of listening which completes the communication of gesture and makes music a reciprocal exchange of information about relationships. This, to me, is as articulate an explanation of the power of recorded music as I have found.

In Small's formulation, there is a value to music measured neither on an individual scale—as in the purchase of analog objects—nor "at scale," as on a digital technology platform. Smart's analysis of music as gesture, and therefore as a form of relational aesthetics, is targeted at the scale of a community. It is the scale of a town. It is precisely the scale that online platforms have failed to maintain, indeed that they actively destroy in their drive to dominate market share.

Yet at root of Smart's argument about value in musicking is something similar to the way tech platforms manufacture wealth: it is likewise based on attention. Platforms strip us of our attention and thereby monetize it at scale. Musicking, in Smart's analysis, pools our attention, which creates a set of relationships vital to community.

If we look at our local businesses that have survived competition from online platforms, they often highlight community. Co-ops, farmers markets, and CSAs (community-supported agriculture) escape online grocery competition because they offer community value apart from price and convenience. The same is true for media—the last general independent bookstore in Harvard Square has survived in part by emphasizing community events with authors that no online retail service can replicate. Similarly, our nonprofit movie theaters sponsor festivals and personal appearances which bring communities of cinephiles together in a manner that streaming cannot. These strategies focus on the audience as much as the "object" on offer. Or to use Christopher Smart's distinction, they make use of verbs rather than merely the noun that defines their business: *growing or sourcing* food, *reading or listening* to books, *sharing or talking* about film.

In music, there has always been an emphasis on performance, as Smart notes. And this no doubt is why live music can survive in the platform era. But the larger community around music is suffering regardless—musicking is more than performance, and most of us engaged in music as a profession are struggling to monetize our work sufficiently to keep producing it. Live original music does not happen in a vacuum, cut off from new recordings.

And new recordings require all kinds of labor that is not compensated by performance, from session playing to arranging to engineering to production to mastering to artwork to publicity to criticism. There are many, many laborers in the community of musicking who cannot claim a portion of any related live music income.

The problem for music, then, is not so different as that for any local store: how to monetize its value for a community sufficiently to withstand devaluation of its goods by the platform economy. This is a problem not only for the supplier of goods but also for the consumer, because if value to a community cannot be realized sufficiently, that value is lost. And ultimately the community itself—organized around these shared values—may dissolve.

What these formulations point to might be termed "a community theory of value." This is distinct from a public good, like a park or education or clean water or sanitation or anything else that a society agrees should be available to all. A community theory of value is based instead on circles that find value where others might find little to none. For nearly all the world, it matters not that my neighborhood fish store and most of my neighborhood book and record stores have closed. But for my neighborhood it is a significant loss of value—not real estate value (which in Cambridge has only gone up during this period, compounding the problem for local stores), or purchasing power (we can all now go online and exercise that power just as well as, if not better than, before). It is a loss of value to the neighborhood *as a community.*

It may seem as if we have no mechanism for measuring community value and thereby monetizing it. But in fact I see it exercised in my daily life as a working musician—and not just in performance, as Christopher Smart emphasized, but also in my work as a recording artist.

Ever since recorded music was digitized in the 1990s, all of us in music have been engaged with piracy as much as any other form of exchange. Not only was a CD easily copied, like the cassette tape that preceded it, but once inserted into a computer it dissolved into digital files that were indistinguishable from the original. When commercial CDs first came on the market, the music industry tried to hide this fact by obfuscating the difference between a "digital master" and an ordinary CD. In fact there is no difference in digital media between a copy and its master, and that became clear to many immediately.

In this regard, you might see all payments for recorded music since digitization as voluntary. The option for a free download of digital music is always there, and has been ever since Napster introduced file sharing in 1999. I myself continue to use file sharing—primarily for difficult-to-find releases, but I have to admit I also turn to it for convenience and economy. I'm obviously far from alone; file sharing only works if there is a critical mass of users.

And yet we musicians do continue to sell copies of our recorded music. Physical media have the added benefit of artwork—which, like a band T-shirt, has become a kind of branded merchandise item divorced from the music itself. (We all know that many who buy LPs today will listen to the music digitally regardless.) But since the advent of streaming, downloads have become even harder to sell than physical media. In 2022, according to the Recording Industry Association of America (RIAA), LPs and CDs managed to eke out 11 percent of the recorded music market in the United States. Downloads added up to only 3 percent.

This remaining sliver of the market—3 percent of recorded music revenue—can only be seen as voluntary at this juncture. Why else pay for a download today? The dominant store supplying them, iTunes, hardly exists any longer now that Apple favors its streaming service Apple Music instead. And the iPod—that dominant consumer technology for listening to downloads—has been discontinued. It is in fact harder now to find a working dedicated digital music player than it is a turntable.

For my own music, paid downloads today come almost exclusively from the platform Bandcamp. And on Bandcamp, I inadvertently ran a kind of experiment regarding pricing and value. In the wake of the 2016 U.S. election, when many in our community were reeling from the results, my partner Naomi and I posted a compilation of B-sides and other miscellaneous tracks on Bandcamp and offered it for free. The album, titled *Spirit of Love* after a song by 1960s band C.O.B., was meant precisely in that way: a gift in the spirit of love for a community we felt could use as much of it as possible.

It is remarkable that Bandcamp allows musicians to donate work to their community in this way—after all, Bandcamp's income depends on a share of payments for downloads, so free exchanges earn it nothing (Bandcamp does not sell ads or consumer data, as other "free" music platforms do). However, Bandcamp offers an option that it urges musicians to use instead of making music purely free: name your price. When downloads are made under these terms, even if the purchasers choose "$0," Bandcamp provides certain privileges to the "buyers," like adding the download to their official "Bandcamp collection" (playable via an app, and viewable by others if shared), and inviting them to post public comments about it on the album's page. Compulsorily free downloads—for example, promotional copies without any payment option—do not include these perks.

So Naomi and I decided to offer our gift download to the community as "name your price, no minimum"—which is how our experiment started accidentally. To our complete surprise, this album of B-sides without a price proceeded to generate more income for us than any of our prior Bandcamp releases.

The gesture—to use Christopher Smart's terminology—was complete. We offered a gift to our community; and the community responded in kind with voluntary payments. What else could we do but remove prices on all Damon & Naomi albums? And our Bandcamp income started to rise across the board . . . We have never looked back. Our albums remain pay-as-you-wish at Bandcamp, and Bandcamp continues to generate meaningful income for our work as recording musicians.

Might it be that our relationship to audience via Bandcamp is based on the kinds of gestures that Christopher Smart describes as musicking, while our relationship to audience via Spotify is not? This would correspond to two distinct types of value: streaming makes use of the platform economy's monetization of attention at scale, while voluntary payments for downloads represent value to a given community.

Both these transactions are virtual; neither solves the problem of scale that is gutting economic life in so many of our cities and towns. But if we put the connections of the internet to work building community rather than tearing it apart, I have confidence that communities will reorganize themselves in physical space too.

9 the next gig

Sound matters to the corporations dominating the digital music industry—at present Spotify, Apple, Amazon and YouTube—as a means to an end. They use sound to attract users. The material of the sound itself is secondary, or even irrelevant, to their business models. This stands in contrast to the traditional power centers of the music industry: the major record labels, for all their wide-ranging bad behaviors toward musicians, depend upon the specific sounds we make. Musicians don't have a great history with the executives running their industry. But with the shift to online platforms, the situation has gone from bad to much worse because we are no longer even working with the primary material our employers need.

In this regard, the corporations engaged in streaming audio are not dissimilar from those generating noise pollution. Sound is a by-product of the most polluting industries in the oceans: shipping, extractive mining, the military. None is in business to make sound. On land, it's no different. Vehicles, construction, compressors, engines of all kinds are rarely used to generate sound deliberately—yet they all do, all the time. Our soundscape is dominated by noisy, profitable activities that are disconnected from the materiality of sound.

This is the crisis in sound we face now, as participants in an increasingly inhospitable physical environment and as a digital media culture. Sound is largely controlled by those who see no value in it. It is at best treated as ancillary to their primary activities, at worst as a waste product.

And yet sound matters. To all of us, though not to all of us in the same manner. Its value is defined by community, and communities are defined by difference. Sound, we might say, relates better to the concept of "multitude" as described by political theorists Michael Hardt and Antonio Negri, than it does to traditional liberal ideas of individualism and the human condition, or to traditional Marxist ideas of class and the masses. The multitude, according to Hardt and Negri, "is not unified but remains plural and multiple . . . a set of *singularities* . . . whose difference cannot be reduced to sameness."[1] Sound, as Christopher Smart observed about music, engenders community through gesture. A church bell rings, or a muezzin calls to a particular audience within audible reach. Music reaches subcultures—whether through performance, broadcast, or recording—that complete the communication of its gestures.

These subcultures based on sound are examples of singularities, as I understand the term—"singularities that act in common." Hardt and Negri's multitude is not made up of isolated individuals, nor is it a unified "people." In their optimistic formulation, the multitude "is an internally different, multiple social subject whose constitution and action is based not on identity or unity (or, much less, indifference) but on what it has in common."[2]

Sound is a material we share in common, yet its value is not universal—it is realized in and by discrete communities. Could there be a more apt illustration of what Hardt and Negri meant by multitude than our collective relationship to sound?

The reason these theorists sought to explain the concept of multitude is they believe "the multitude is the only social subject capable of realizing democracy, that is, the rule of everyone by everyone. The stakes, in other words, are extremely high."[3] Their larger political argument is that opposition to global capital needs a different organization than in previous eras, because labor is no longer either industrial or agricultural, and no longer necessarily unified by workplace. Today, as so many experience, work may be a "gig," and its product may be immaterial. Exactly what we musicians have always faced.

In the twentieth century, music was often seen as an outlier to typical forms of labor—singing about John Henry was distinct from being John Henry. But today, music is emblematic of many

The Next Gig 97

contemporary forms of work. It fits the description of "post-Fordism" labor, which, as Hardt and Negri explain, is "flexible, mobile and precarious":

> *Flexible* because workers have to adapt to different tasks, *mobile* because workers have to move frequently between jobs, and *precarious* because no contracts guarantee stable, long-term employment.[4]

Music also fits the model of immaterial labor, often used to describe the information economy where rather than producing physical goods, the "key characteristics [are] to produce communication, social relations, and cooperation." Indeed, music excels at an aspect of immaterial labor that Hardt and Negri look to as a basis for resistance via the multitude:

> The difference of immaterial labor . . . is that its products are themselves, in many respects, immediately social and common. Producing communication, affective relationships, and knowledges, in contrast to cars and typewriters, can directly expand the realm of what we share in common.[5]

Immaterial labor—like music—increases the common, even though its forms are various and our lives as workers in it isolated due to the gig economy. Hardt and Negri see sharing in the common of the multitude as building a collective resistance to consolidated capital. Music can help make this argument real *if it is seen as work.* Advocacy for musicians' rights to fair treatment is connected to the struggle against irresponsible corporate behavior at large, as power concentrates in the hands of fewer and fewer actors. The fresh wave of unionization we are witnessing in many industries today is a powerful response to this consolidation. Yet at present, musicians are largely barred from following suit due to labor laws accommodating outdated ideas of our form of production.

The music industry is particularly, notoriously consolidated. There are only three major labels left (Universal, Warner, and Sony). There are five platforms that control 80 percent of subscription streaming, globally (Spotify, Apple, Amazon, Tencent, and Google). And there are just two promoters responsible for 90 percent of the live music industry (Live Nation and AEG).

Still there are loads of musicians working everywhere, playing musics that don't even have Billboard charts, much less make them with a bullet. There are loads of music labels apart from the majors, and music promoters outside Live Nation and AEG. The business is in truth so much bigger, and broader, and more diverse than the "industry." It is a network of singularities, producing commonality.

I've heard many times that organizing musicians is like herding cats. And yes, there are reasons for the cliché. But there are also reasons why musicians form bands. Even if many of these are doomed to fall apart—all those cats with instruments—music by definition embraces the idea of collectivity.

When all our touring calendars went blank in March 2020 because of the COVID pandemic, I think many musicians dove into Zoom out of pure reflex; it was like looking for a place to hang out after soundcheck. We are used to killing time, and we're accustomed to doing that together.

Zoom turns out to be a lousy place for music, though. The company boasts that in the digital conference industry, their software has the lowest latency—the delay between an action and when it registers on the screen—and that it never exceeds 150 milliseconds. This sounds good until you find out that for music, the maximum workable latency is generally considered to be 10 milliseconds, beyond which the cues between musicians break down. (As a drummer, I find even 10 too much; a few milliseconds here or there can have a lot to do with feel, swing, groove.) This isn't just being fussy—try clapping along with your own image on Zoom, and I guarantee you won't even be able to keep time with yourself.

But ever since that initial lockdown, I have been hanging out on Zoom with musicians and *not* playing music. Instead, we've been doing what Zoom was designed for: conferencing. This is a new activity for most of us. Musicians generally don't have business meetings, at least not with one another. What happens when you put us in a virtual conference room together? The result, it turns out, is the same as what happens when you gather any group of workers under the same roof: we organize.

United Musicians and Allied Workers (UMAW) could probably only have started in a year without touring. Normally, musicians who don't regularly play together tend to meet only briefly, momentarily crossing paths when we share a bill or pass through one another's hometowns. We're too itinerant to schedule regular get-togethers; there are professional roadies who don't even bother having a permanent address, just a mailbox at a post office in a state without income tax. But with all of us stuck at home, scheduling regular Zoom meetings was easy. Musicians contacted other musicians. We met to talk about the situation we'd found ourselves in and what we might do about it.

At the first meetings, I knew only a few people in the virtual room—mostly the members of Downtown Boys, a political punk band I like a lot. There were others I knew from their music, though we'd never met: Sadie Dupuis from the band Speedy Ortiz, Ryan Mahan from Algiers, Enongo Lumumba-Kasongo, or SAMMUS, Cole Smith from DIIV. There were also many whose music I would learn about as I got to know them through these virtual gatherings. Musicians are quick at forming bonds. I think the intensity of our relationships mirrors the intensity of our work; you get to know someone very well and very fast in the confines of a green room or van.

Soon we were comparing notes on our economic lives. Over the past fifteen years—ever since streaming took hold—the only real income many of us can earn from our music is through performance. When the pandemic shut down venues it threw us all out of work, just as surely as it did the staff at every bar, club, and theater any of us has ever played. Musicians continued to make music, of course; many of us even managed to write, record, and release new material during lockdown. But few of us had any hope of earning much money from that labor. In order to earn the equivalent of a fifteen dollars-per-hour job from Spotify, you'd need 833,334 streams of your music per month—for each person in your band. And that's only if you're self-releasing your recordings. If you have a label deal, you'll likely need at least twice that number.

Attracting millions of streams per month is possible, but not likely. And typically, those proceeds need to be shared not just with a label but with producers, managers, publicists—all the labor it takes to create a recording and get it heard. You might need tens, even hundreds of millions of plays per month to make a living wage, something only the very top of the industry's pyramid can expect from streaming.

This state of affairs will be painfully familiar to workers in many industries. Musicians are, after all, the original gig workers: like Uber drivers, we're independent contractors who bear the cost of our own tools, materials, healthcare, and self-employment taxes. Meanwhile, the corporations that control access to our work collect billions in revenue.

Thanks to the accident of lockdown, we at UMAW did what organized workers before us have done. We researched our industry's structure, discussed what it means for us individually, and formulated plans to assert our collective interest—things we would never have been able to do from the back of a van. Our first action was to join other more experienced organizations in successfully lobbying Congress to include gig workers in pandemic unemployment assistance. The second, launched in October 2020, was a public campaign called Justice at Spotify: a set of demands for the company to include musicians' economic interests in their goals and practices. Like all labor organizations, we are asking for a seat at the table where crucial decisions are made about our industry and our welfare. And since the streaming platforms have not yet relented, we have now drafted a bill and asked Congress to get involved. The Living Wage for Musicians Act was introduced by Rep. Rashida Tlaib and Rep. Jamaal Bowman to the House of Representatives in March 2024 and has been referred to the Judiciary Committee for consideration. It would regulate streaming and for the first time guarantee direct payments from the platforms to recording musicians.

Working with other musicians to build UMAW has, for me, been an uplifting experience in what could be very depressing times. Many of the other members are close to half my age, and I've been continually inspired by their energy, their care for one another, their fury at injustice. Passions have sometimes spilled over, same as they do in bands, but the way these younger musicians model both giving and demanding respect is something I don't remember learning so well anywhere else—definitely not as a part of my era's indie-rock scene, anyway.

It's been a joy to have this new space for hanging out with other musicians. On occasion, meetings have turned into discussions of how important the social aspect of organizing has become for us. Musicians are, almost to a one, very social beings—that's why we form bands! And we have discovered that we can work together in other ways, too.

This book began at soundcheck in a basement club in an alley in Harvard Square. I want to close it at another gig, of sorts, just around the corner—outdoors on the appropriately named Cambridge Common.

It was there that I found myself thinking about the ties between music and labor at a rally with Senator Bernie Sanders of Vermont, Sara Nelson of the Association of Flight Attendants–CWA, and Sean O'Brien of the International Brotherhood of Teamsters, who had come to town together just like a group of touring bands. It was a beautiful summer day, and the spirit in the crowd was not unlike at a small music festival—the kind where you still recognize people from your particular scene, but big enough that you see a lot of new faces from other scenes you're not privy to.

In this case, the new faces for me were the Teamsters: UPS hats, a "South Boston Viet-Nam Memorial" T-shirt with local Chapter 25 logo in a green clover, and lots of very big shoulders. I'm sure the socialist crowd with their black shorts and earnest badges were new to the Teamsters, too. And then there were the nurses, flight attendants, MIT grad students, Starbucks baristas . . . each involved in distinct local labor fights. The overriding message was solidarity: "Fighting Back Against Corporate Greed," as the rally poster read. And the audience response to all the speakers was loud. As loud as at a music festival.

Sara Nelson, international president of the Association of Flight Attendants–CWA, spoke first, with a positive message about collective power:

> If we want to change this world, we start by organizing where capital exists—in our workplaces. . . . Working people—when we stand together, when we have each others' back—have the power to change this world, and get what we need. The billionaires will keep going. But even on those dick rockets that they build to go out into space while they leave the rest of us burning on this earth, even there, there are flight attendants on those rockets who asked us if we could help them unionize. We are one, and we are everywhere.[6]

Musicians, too, have always organized in their workplaces—even if we work in very small units. Bands spend a lot of time talking with one another and to all the music workers we come in contact with through the course of our days and nights, load-in to load-out. Talking *is* organizing. We share ideas about how the world works, and how our art functions in it.

Scenes—bands that are drawn to one another, fans of bands that are drawn to one another, labels that are drawn to the bands and the fans who are drawn to one another, venues at the center of these communities—combine to create another level of organizing. Again, there's always a lot of talk. Sharing information, sharing ideas, sharing complaints . . . I think any traditional workplace organizer would recognize the way music scenes coalesce and take on a collective direction.

Can we combine disparate scenes, like the rally I was attending? That's a level of solidarity we don't always see in music. Festivals and award ceremonies might gather multiple scenes together, but the time is brief, the situation provisional, the structure typically corporate and competitive. Perhaps the problem isn't really herding cats—it's that when we find ourselves all together, we're at a fancy cat show.

Sean O'Brien, general president of the International Brotherhood of Teamsters, spoke next. He delivered tough talk about CEOs who aren't listening to their workers:

> Let's get back to the three stooges: Bezos, Musk, and Sgt. Schultz from Starbucks. There has never been a more inspiring time for organized labor, and for people to organize within their workplaces. Because of those three nitwits and their bad behavior, they're actually helping us organize, they're helping us mobilize, they're helping us strategize—and they don't know it. Because when employers treat workers bad, we—organized labor, unions—are the only option to hold these white-collar crime syndicates known as

The Next Gig 105

corporate America accountable. And when we organize, we strategize—especially with the Amazon, the Starbucks workers. Never been so proud in my life, to see a youth movement start to organize.

Musicians interested in organizing have also been given an unlikely boost by the tech platforms which dominate our industry. Like other clumsily rapacious billionaires eating up the economy, Spotify's CEO Daniel Ek is a gift to cat herders. Ek has angered musicians time and again with widely ridiculed statements such as, "Today . . . the cost of creating content [is] close to zero."[7] The streaming platforms' bad faith toward musicians—*all* musicians—is uniting us across scenes. And just as Sean O'Brien of the Teamsters observed, the behavior of these corporations and their CEOs makes clear that we are in need of a way to hold them accountable. How are any of us on our own to deal with Spotify, much less Amazon, Apple, or Google? These are among the richest and most powerful companies on the planet. Our only option, whether we were ever drawn to it before or not, is to organize.

Senator Bernie Sanders spoke in the headline slot, and delivered the big picture:

> We have the moral responsibility to be outraged when three people own more wealth than half of American society, when the top 1 percent are earning 45 percent of all incomes, when corporate CEOs are now making 350 times what their workers are making. . . . What we are seeing today is something extraordinary. We are seeing a rebirth of the American trade union movement from coast to coast. We're talking about blue-collar workers, we're talking about white-collar workers, we're talking about young

people, we're talking about older people, all across the sector. Growing the union movement gives us economic power, gives us dignity, gives us respect on the job—but it gives us something more. . . . One of the things that the media tells us every single day, it tells us through politicians, through corporate leaders, it says: think small, not big. . . . At best maybe, maybe you'll get a little thing. And we say: the hell with that. We're thinking big.

Here's the twist that takes this big, as Bernie says. Because once we organize across scenes—once we've enlarged our idea of solidarity in music, from a single band to a group of sympathetic bands to all recording artists to workers in other industries—then, with a truly big voice, we can demand big changes.

I firmly believe that if musicians demand big changes, not only will our economic conditions improve but the environment at large will benefit because the material we work with is sound. And if Michael Hardt and Antonio Negri are right about the multitude, democracy itself may well benefit.

At the close of the rally, with a flourish, Bernie cited Woody Guthrie ("This land is our land!"), and walked off to exit music by John Lennon and the Plastic Ono Band: "Power to the People."

notes

ONE: LOAD-IN

1. UK Music, *This Is Music 2022,* https://www.ukmusic.org/wp-content/uploads/2022/09/This-Is-Music-2022-Spreads.pdf (accessed March 29, 2025).

2. Thanks to James Keelaghan for allowing me to share his story of Eugene Peck's guitar in this chapter.

3. Caitlin Kizielewicz, "Music Streaming Consumption Fell During COVID-19 Lockdowns," July 15, 2021, Carnegie Mellon University News, https://www.cmu.edu/news/stories/archives/2021/july/music-streaming-down-during-pandemic.html.

TWO: SOUND IS A MATERIAL

1. Rachel Carson, *Silent Spring* (1962; Boston: Mariner Books, 2002), 103.

2. Sabrina Imbler, "In the Oceans, the Volume Is Rising as Never Before, *New York Times,* February 4, 2021 (updated July 9, 2021), https://www.nytimes.com/2021/02/04/science/ocean-marine-noise-pollution.html; Carlos M. Duarte et al., "The Soundscape of the Anthropocene

Ocean," *Science* 371, no. 6529 (February 5, 2021), https://www.science.org/doi/10.1126/science.aba4658.

3. Duarte et al., "The Soundscape of the Anthropocene Ocean." Further quotations are from this article.

4. Krause quoted in Rachel Nuwer, "The Last Place on Earth Without Human Noise," January 16, 2014, BBC, https://www.bbc.com/future/article/20140117-earths-last-place-without-noise.

5. "Quiet Places," Quiet Parks International, https://www.quietparks.org/quiet-places (accessed March 29, 2025); Les Blomberg, "Noise Pollution in the 21st Century," May 7, 2014, presented at the 167th Acoustical Society of America Meeting, https://acoustics.org/pressroom/httpdocs/167th/3aID2_Blomberg.html.

6. Bill McKibben, *The End of Nature* (1989; New York: Random House, 2006), 40.

7. Francesco Aletta, "Listening to Cities: From Noisy Environments to Positive Soundscapes," UN Environment Programme Frontiers 2022 Report, 2, https://wedocs.unep.org/bitstream/handle/20.500.11822/38060/Frontiers_2022CH1.pdf.

8. Ibid., 3.

9. J. Ballester et al., "Heat-related Mortality in Europe During the Summer of 2022," *Nature Medicine* 29, nos. 1857–66 (2023), available at https://www.nature.com/articles/s41591-023-02419-z; UNICEF, "New Study Finds That 43,000 'Excess Deaths' May Have Occurred in 2022 from the Drought in Somalia," March 20, 2023, UNICEF press release, https://www.unicef.org/press-releases/new-study-finds-43000-excess-deaths-may-have-occurred-2022-drought-somalia.

10. Kim Velsey, "All the Quiet Money Can Buy: Talking to the Professional Soundproofers for the Ultrarich," August 9, 2023, Curbed (*New York* magazine), https://www.curbed.com/2023/08/professional-soundproofers-rich-luxury-condos-dumbo-windows.html.

11. Shannon Osaka, "How Air Conditioners Will Have to Change in the Future," *Washington Post,* June 9, 2023, available at https://www.

washingtonpost.com/climate-environment/2023/06/07/air-conditioners-humid-climate-change/.

12. See Tom Haynes, "Heat Pumps 'Too Noisy' for Millions of British Homes, Government Told," *Telegraph,* November 12, 2023, available at https://www.telegraph.co.uk/money/net-zero/heat-pumps-noisy-millions-british-homes/.

13. Elizabeth Kolbert, "Where Have All the Insects Gone?" *National Geographic* (May 2020), available at https://www.nationalgeographic.com/magazine/article/where-have-all-the-insects-gone-feature; Caspar A. Hallmann et al., "More Than 75 Percent Decline over 27 Years in Total Flying Insect Biomass in Protected Areas," *PLOS ONE* (October 18, 2017), available at https://journals.plos.org/plosone/article?id=10.1371/journal.pone.0185809; James Ashworth, "UK's Flying Insects Have Declined by 60% in 20 Years," *Natural History Museum* (May 6, 2022), https://www.nhm.ac.uk/discover/news/2022/may/uks-flying-insects-have-declined-60-in-20-years.html; Lawrence Ball, Robbie Still, Alison Riggs, et al., "Technical Report: The Bugs Matter Citizen Science Survey: Counting Insect 'Splats' on Vehicle Number Plates Reveals a 58.5% Reduction in the Abundance of Actively Flying Insects in the UK Between 2004 and 2021," Bugs Matter 2021 National Report, https://cdn.buglife.org.uk/2022/05/Bugs-Matter-2021-National-Report.pdf (accessed March 29, 2025).

FOUR: SOUND HAS VALUE

1. Ashley Carman, "Spotify Looked to Ban White Noise Podcasts to Become More Profitable," Bloomberg, August 17, 2023, https://www.bloomberg.com/news/newsletters/2023-08-17/white-noise-podcasters-are-costing-spotify-38-million-a-year.

2. Jonathan Sterne, *The Audible Past* (Durham, N.C.: Duke University Press, 2003), 332.

3. BAFTA, "The Making of Planet Earth II," May 14, 2017, YouTube, https://www.youtube.com/watch?v=F7P8MAL4H0k.

4. Insider, "How Sounds Are Faked for Nature Documentaries" December 24, 2020, YouTube, https://www.youtube.com/watch?v=AcmhWs7HMIc.

5. Charles Bernstein, "How Poetry Survives," *Baffler*, no. 6 (December 1994), https://thebaffler.com/salvos/how-poetry-survives.

6. R. Murray Schafer, "The Music of the Environment," in *Audio Culture: Readings in Modern Music*, ed. Christoph Cox and Daniel Warner (New York: Continuum, 2004), 37.

7. Edgard Varèse, "The Electronic Medium (1962)," in *Audio Culture*, ed. Christoph Cox (New York: Continuum, 2004).

8. Mark Roland, "Chris Watson," *Electronic Sound* 79 (2021): 37.

9. Bernie Krause and United Visual Artists, *The Great Animal Orchestra: A Work from the Collection of the Fondation Cartier pour l'art contemporain* (Paris: Fondation Cartier, 2019), 83.

10. Wild Sanctuary, https://www.wildsanctuary.com/ (accessed March 29, 2025).

11. Krause and United Visual Artists, *The Great Animal Orchestra*, 35.

12. Luke Turner, "Chris Watson on Recording the Music of the Natural World," Quietus, January 24, 2013, https://thequietus.com/interviews/things-i-have-learned/chris-watson-interview-sound-recording-cabaret-voltaire/.

13. Roland, "Chris Watson, 37.

14. Matthew Blackwell, "Chris Watson," Tone Glow 57 (March 22, 2021), https://toneglow.substack.com/p/057-chris-watson.

FIVE: BACKSTAGE

1. Walter J. Ong, *Orality and Literacy* (London: Methuen, 1982), 31.

2. Ibid., 134.

SIX: MUSIC IS LABOR

1. "Company Pay Ratios," AFL-CIO Executive Paywatch, http://web.archive.org/web/20230930103142/https:/aflcio.org/paywatch/company-pay-ratios (accessed September 30, 2023).

2. Amy K. Glasmeier, "Living Wage Calculator," Living Wage Institute, February 1, 2023, https://livingwage.mit.edu/articles/103-new-data-posted-2023-living-wage-calculator.

3. "Musicians' Census Financial Insight Report." September 2023, p. 7, Musicians' Census 2023, https://static1.squarespace.com/static/6398a2cf26f9de4e45e94dd7/t/64fae3635773f313b194d963/1694163834806/MC23+Report+0923.pdf.

4. Matt Padley and Juliet Stone, "A Minimum Income Standard for the United Kingdom in 2023," September 8, 2023, Centre for Research in Social Policy, Loughborough University, https://www.jrf.org.uk/a-minimum-income-standard-for-the-united-kingdom-in-2023.

5. Human Artistry Campaign, "Core Principles for Artificial Intelligence Applications in Support of Human Creativity and Accomplishment," https://www.humanartistrycampaign.com/ (accessed March 29, 2025).

6. Holly+, https://holly.mirror.xyz/54ds2IiOnvthjGFkokFCoaI4EabytH9xjAYy1irHy94.

7. Emily Zemler, "Mitski Asks Fans to Put Their Phones away During Her Upcoming Shows." *Rolling Stone* (February 25, 2022), https://www.rollingstone.com/music/music-news/mitski-phones-statement-tour-1312596/.

8. Chris DeVille, "Big Thief to Concertgoers: Please Stop Talking During the Opening Set," Stereogum (April 20, 2022), https://www.stereogum.com/2184022/big-thief-adrianne-lenker-please-stop-talking-during-the-opening-set/news/.

9. Jacques Rancière, "The Concept of 'Critique' and the 'Critique of Political Economy,' " in *Reading Capital: The Complete Edition,* ed. Louis Althusser et al. (New York: Verso, 2015), 119.

10. Diane Elson, "The Value Theory of Labour," *Value: The Representation of Labour in Capitalism,* ed. Diane Elson (Atlantic Highlands, N.J.: Humanities Press, 1979).

11. Maria Eriksson et al., *Spotify Teardown: Inside the Black Box of Streaming Music* (Cambridge: MIT Press, 2019), 165.

EIGHT: A COMMUNITY THEORY OF VALUE

1. Charles C. Matthews, "Cambridge Stacks," *Harvard Crimson* (June 23, 1985), https://www.thecrimson.com/article/1985/6/23/cambridge-stacks-pwhere-there-are-cafes/; Lewis Burke Frumkes, "At Cambridge, Bookstores in Volume." *New York Times,* May 7, 1989, https://www.nytimes.com/1989/05/07/travel/shoppers-world-at-cambridge-bookstores-in-volume.html.

2. See Daniel Sanchez, "Spotify Leases Even More Office Space at the World Trade Center," September 24, 2018, Digital Music News, https://www.digitalmusicnews.com/2018/09/24/latest-spotify-4-wtc-additional-office-space/; Pavel Ibarra Meda, "Spotify Camp Nou is Barcelona Stadium's Official New Name," September 2, 2022, Marca, https://www.marca.com/en/football/barcelona/2022/02/09/6203037a268e3e6d148b4591.html; Katherine Rosman et al., "Spotify Bet Big on Joe Rogan. It Got More Than It Counted On," *New York Times,* February 17, 2022. https://www.nytimes.com/2022/02/17/arts/music/spotify-joe-rogan-misinformation.html.

3. Christopher Small, *Musicking* (Middletown, Conn.: Wesleyan University Press, 1998), 218.

NINE: THE NEXT GIG

Portions of this chapter were previously published in *The New York Times Magazine.*

1. Michael Hardt and Antonio Negri, *Multitude* (New York: Penguin, 2004), 99.

2. Ibid., 100.

3. Ibid.

4. Ibid., 112.

5. Ibid., 113, 114.

6. For a video of the rally see "The Working Class: Fighting Back Against Corporate Greed. Rally in Boston, Sunday, August 21 [2022]," YouTube, https://www.youtube.com/live/vsgMs-xmXHc?feature=shared (accessed March 29, 2025).

7. Marco Quiroz-Guitirrez, "Spotify's CEO Got Roasted by artists After he said the Cost of Creating Content Is 'Close to Zero.' Now He's Trying to Walk Back His 'Clumsy' Remark," June 3, 2024, Fortune, https://fortune.com/2024/06/03/spotify-ceo-daniel-ek-content-cost-close-to-zero-stearming-subscription-fee-hike/.

Damon Krukowski is an indie rock musician (Galaxie 500, Damon & Naomi), and writes the newsletter Dada Drummer Almanach. He is author of *The New Analog: Listening and Reconnecting in a Digital World* (2017) and *Ways of Hearing* (2019), which was adapted from a Radiotopia podcast series of the same name. He has also written about sound and music for many publications including *Artforum, Art in America,* the *New Yorker,* the *Guardian, Pitchfork,* and the *Wire.*

Featuring intriguing pairings of authors and subjects, each volume in the Why X Matters series presents a concise argument for the continuing relevance of an important idea.

Also in the series

Why Acting Matters	David Thomson
Why Architecture Matters	Paul Goldberger
Why Arendt Matters	Elisabeth Young-Bruehl
Why Argument Matters	Lee Siegel
Why Baseball Matters	Susan Jacoby
Why the Constitution Matters	Mark Tushnet
Why the Dreyfus Affair Matters	Louis Begley
Why the Museum Matters	Daniel H. Weiss
Why the New Deal Matters	Eric Rauchway
Why Niebuhr Matters	Charles Lemert
Why Poetry Matters	Jay Parini
Why Preservation Matters	Max Page
Why the Romantics Matter	Peter Gay
Why Translation Matters	Edith Grossman
Why Trilling Matters	Adam Kirsch
Why Writing Matters	Nicholas Delbanco